Light & Easy Meals

ARMOUR®
LOWER SALT*

CONTENTS

First published in the United States of America in 1989 by The Mallard Press. All rights reserved.

This edition was prepared by Evenson & Associates for Armour Food Company, Omaha, Nebraska 68102.

Recipe Development: Cheryl K. Evenson and Barbara J. Torres
Project Coordinator: Evenson & Associates
Photography: Robert Ervin Photography, Inc.
Food Stylist: Cheryl K. Evenson
Accessories Stylists: Barbara J. Torres and Cheryl K. Evenson
Nutritional Analysis: Marsha Viers, registered dietitian

Produced by Publications International, Ltd., Lincolnwood, IL.

Manufactured in Yugoslavia

h g f e d c b a

ISBN: 0-792-45113-9

Pictured on front cover: Ham Pasta Primavera (page 39).

Pictured on back cover (left, top to bottom): Puff Pastry Pizza (page 16), Hot Dog Chili (page 40) and German Pancake with Bacon (page 66). (Right): Bacon Nachos (page 64).

MALLARD
PRESS

MALLARD PRESS
An Imprint of BDD Promotional Book Company, Inc.
666 Fifth Avenue
New York, N.Y. 10103

FOREWORD

By Armand E. Brodeur, M.D.

We've all heard the same advice over and over again from our physicians, "You need to cut down on the amount of salt in your diet." When you lower your sodium intake, it can help control high blood pressure and can reduce your risk of coronary heart disease. Most physicians recommend a daily sodium intake of 1100 mg to 3300 mg.

I know that lowering your sodium intake can be challenging, especially since today's convenience foods are excessively high in sodium. I also realize that changing current eating habits isn't easy. But you owe it to yourself, and your heart, to make the effort. I recommend the following dietary and lifestyle changes to achieve better health. For greater success, incorporate only one change at a time into your life.

- Try new recipes with reduced salt and leave the salt shaker off the table.
- Learn how to read food labels when shopping. (Sodium should be listed near the end of the ingredients.)
- Exercise regularly and lose weight if overweight.
- Reduce cholesterol and fat, but get adequate amounts of calcium and potassium.
- Limit alcohol intake and avoid excessive amounts of caffeine.
- Quit smoking, avoid stress and learn to relax.

Now you ask, "How can I cut down on sodium and still enjoy the foods I like?" We are all busy people and really don't have the time to learn how to cook a different way. Today's food manufacturers are helping you eat healthier by offering many products that have a reduced sodium content or have no salt added. This makes it easier for you to make changes.

Armour Food Company is one of these manufacturers. They offer you lower salt meat and cheese products that have the same great taste as their regular products. I recommend them. They can be a part of the answer to your sodium reduction program.

Cardinal Glennon Children's Hospital in St. Louis is one of the leading pediatric medical centers in the country and a pioneer in developing lifelong nutrition programs. Dr. Brodeur, director emeritus at Cardinal Glennon, dispenses medical advice to millions of people each year through his daily medical radio show, many lectures and television appearances. Dr. Brodeur is also the medical consultant to Armour Food Company.

INTRODUCTION

We at Armour Food Company know that more people than ever before are concerned with healthier living and eating—but today's busy lifestyles don't leave much time for meal planning and preparation. This book was designed to provide you and your family with recipes that are easy-to-prepare, tasty and healthful.

Reducing the amount of salt in your diet is an important step to take toward healthier eating. Armour Lower Salt ham, bacon, hot dogs and cheeses are sensible alternatives for those of you who want to cut down on the amount of salt you eat each day. These products have significantly less salt than our regular products, yet taste so good that every member of your family will enjoy them—not just those who are restricting their sodium intakes.

Although all the recipes in this book provide less than 740 milligrams of sodium per serving, they are *not* intended for people on strict sodium-restricted diets. Contact your physician if you have any questions concerning your diet.

Nutritional Analysis: Nutrition information is given for each recipe. This information was computed for the food items in the ingredient list. When more than one ingredient choice is listed, the first ingredient was used for the analysis. Food items in the recipes that are designated by "if desired" are *not* included in the analysis. When a range is given for the number of servings in the recipe, the analysis was computed according to the largest number of servings.

Microwave Cooking: All microwave directions were tested in a countertop microwave oven rated at 700 watts. Microwave cooking times are approximate. Numerous variables, such as starting temperature, shape and amount of food, can affect cooking times. Use the cooking times as a guideline and check for doneness before adding more time. Lower wattage ovens may consistently require longer cooking times.

For questions concerning Armour Products, contact: Armour Food Company, Consumer Services Department, One Central Park Plaza, Omaha, NE 68102-1679.

FRENCH TOAST WITH HAM STRIPS

Makes 4 servings

3 eggs, slightly beaten
½ cup skim milk
½ teaspoon vanilla
1 tablespoon unsalted margarine or butter
4 slices whole wheat or white bread
2 cups (8 ounces) Armour Lower Salt Ham cut into 3×¾-inch strips
1 (20-ounce) can lite cherry fruit filling

Combine eggs, milk and vanilla in flat dish. Melt margarine in large skillet over medium heat. Dip bread into egg mixture. Panfry in skillet until golden brown. Turn and brown second side. Brown all sides of ham strips in same skillet with bread slices.

Meanwhile, heat cherry fruit filling in small saucepan over medium heat about 5 to 7 minutes, or until heated through. Place 4 warmed ham strips on top of each French toast slice; top with ½ cup of the warmed cherry sauce. Garnish with parsley, if desired.

NUTRITION INFORMATION PER SERVING:
344 calories, 20.2 g protein, 12.8 g fat, 40.5 g carbohydrates, 234 mg cholesterol, 729 mg sodium.

HAM TORTELLINI SALAD

Makes 6 to 8 servings

1 (7- to 8-ounce) package cheese-filled spinach tortellini
3 cups (12 ounces) Armour Lower Salt Ham cut into ¾-inch cubes
½ cup sliced green onions
10 cherry tomatoes, cut in half
1 cup bottled low sodium, creamy buttermilk *or* reduced calorie zesty Italian salad dressing
Leaf lettuce or butterhead lettuce, washed and drained
¼ cup finely chopped red pepper

Cook tortellini according to package directions omitting salt; drain and run under cold water to cool. Combine all ingredients *except* leaf lettuce and red pepper in large bowl. Toss until well blended. Serve on lettuce-lined salad plates. Sprinkle with red pepper. Serve immediately.

NUTRITION INFORMATION PER SERVING:
164.5 calories, 12.6 g protein, 3.5 g fat, 17.4 g carbohydrates, 38.5 mg cholesterol, 545 mg sodium.

◆◆◆

Look for low sodium, reduced calorie salad dressings in the special diet sections of your local supermarket, or in with the regular salad dressings.

HAM & FRUIT PANCAKE ROLLS

Makes 8 rolled pancakes

2 cups complete pancake mix
8 ounces Armour Lower Salt Ham, thinly sliced
8 tablespoons bottled fruit-flavored applesauce *or* canned lite cherry fruit filling

Prepare pancake mix according to package directions. Spray griddle or large skillet with nonstick cooking spray. Using ⅓ cup measure, pour batter onto hot griddle. Cook as directed on package, making eight 5-inch pancakes. Place 1 ounce of ham on each cooked pancake; top with 1 tablespoon applesauce. Roll up pancake around ham; secure with toothpicks, if needed. Repeat with remaining pancakes. Serve with additional applesauce, if desired.

NUTRITION INFORMATION PER ROLL:
145 calories, 7.2 g protein, 1.9 g fat, 23.6 g carbohydrates, 14 mg cholesterol, 596 mg sodium.

Ham Tortellini Salad

BATTER-DIPPED HAM SANDWICHES

Makes 4 servings

½ cup sliced green onions
7 ounces light cream cheese, softened
8 slices cinnamon bread
4 ounces Armour Lower Salt Ham, thinly sliced
3 eggs
½ cup skim milk
1 teaspoon sugar
4 tablespoons unsalted margarine or butter

Combine green onions with cream cheese in small bowl. Spread mixture evenly over all bread slices. Top each of 4 bread slices with 1 ounce of ham. Top with second slice of bread, cheese side down.

Combine eggs, milk and sugar in flat dish; beat well. Dip each sandwich quickly into egg mixture, turning to coat both sides. Melt margarine in large skillet or griddle over medium-high heat. Cook sandwiches until golden brown on both sides. Garnish with frosted red grapes, if desired.

NUTRITION INFORMATION PER SERVING: 518 calories, 19 g protein, 34.2 g fat, 31 g carbohydrates, 263 mg cholesterol, 709 mg sodium.

◆◆◆

Swirled cinnamon bread makes Batter-Dipped Ham Sandwiches even more attractive.

BRUNCH POTATO CASSOULET

Makes 4 to 6 servings

2 tablespoons unsalted margarine or butter
2 cups (8 ounces) Armour Lower Salt Ham cut into ½-inch cubes
2 cups frozen natural potato wedges
1 cup sliced fresh mushrooms
½ cup chopped red onion
½ cup chopped green pepper
1 cup frozen speckled butter beans, cooked according to package directions omitting salt and drained

Preheat oven to 350°F. Melt margarine in large skillet over medium heat. Add ham, potatoes, mushrooms, onion and green pepper; cook over medium heat about 5 to 6 minutes, or until onion is soft. Stir in cooked beans. Transfer to medium earthenware pot or ovenproof Dutch oven. Bake, covered, about 10 to 12 minutes, or until heated through. If desired, sprinkle with lower salt cheese and broil 4 to 6 inches from heat source about 2 to 3 minutes, or until cheese is melted and slightly browned.

NUTRITION INFORMATION PER SERVING: 161 calories, 10.1 g protein, 6.7 g fat, 14.3 g carbohydrates, 18.6 mg cholesterol, 391 mg sodium.

Brunch Potato Cassoulet

COLORFUL HAM OMELET

Makes 2 servings

3 tablespoons unsalted margarine or butter, divided
¼ cup finely chopped onion
¼ cup *each* finely chopped red and green pepper
½ cup (2 ounces) Armour Lower Salt Ham cut into ¼-inch cubes
6 eggs
¼ cup (1 ounce) shredded Armour Lower Salt Cheddar Cheese

Melt 1 tablespoon of the margarine in small skillet or omelet pan over medium heat. Add onion and red and green peppers; sauté about 3 to 5 minutes, or until tender. Add ham cubes; heat thoroughly. Remove and set aside.

Melt 1 tablespoon of the margarine in same pan over medium heat; add 3 well-beaten eggs. Cook eggs, pulling edges toward center, until almost set. Spoon half of the ham mixture over eggs. Cover and continue cooking until set. *Do not overcook.* Fold half of the omelet over other half. Sprinkle half of the cheese over top. Gently slide onto serving plate. Repeat with remaining ingredients. Serve immediately. Garnish with cilantro, if desired.

MICROWAVE DIRECTIONS:
Place 1 tablespoon of the margarine, onion, red and green peppers, and ham in small microwave-safe dish. Cook on High power for 3 minutes; set aside. Separate eggs; beat egg whites in medium bowl until soft peaks form. Beat egg yolks with 2 tablespoons water in small bowl. Gently fold yolk mixture into whites. Melt remaining 2 tablespoons margarine in microwave-safe 9-inch pie plate; swirl to coat bottom. Carefully pour half of the egg mixture into pie plate. Cook on Medium power (50%) about 7 to 9 minutes or until almost set. Spoon half of the ham mixture and cheese over eggs. Cook on Medium-High power (70%) for 2 more minutes, or until eggs are set. Fold and remove omelet from pie plate as above. Repeat with remaining ingredients. Garnish as above.

NUTRITION INFORMATION PER SERVING: 497 calories, 27 g protein, 42 g fat, 6.4 g carbohydrates, 851 mg cholesterol, 500 mg sodium.

Top: Cornmeal Bacon Shortcakes (page 12); bottom: Colorful Ham Omelet

CORNMEAL BACON SHORTCAKES

Makes 6 shortcakes or muffins

1¼ cups all-purpose flour
¾ cup cornmeal
2 tablespoons sugar
1½ tablespoons low sodium
  baking powder
¾ cup unsalted margarine or
  butter, cold
12 slices Armour Lower Salt
  Bacon, cooked crisp and
  finely crumbled
⅓ cup skim milk
1 egg

Preheat oven to 400°F. Combine flour, cornmeal, sugar and baking powder. Cut in margarine until mixture is crumbly. Stir in bacon. Add milk and egg; stir until just moistened. Do not overmix. Spray 6 shortcake or muffin tin cups with nonstick cooking spray. Spoon ⅓ cup of the batter into each cup. Bake about 10 to 12 minutes, or until golden brown. Garnish with fresh basil, if desired.

NUTRITION INFORMATION PER CAKE: 452 calories, 9.7 g protein, 30.6 g fat, 39.5 g carbohydrates, 57.7 mg cholesterol, 271 mg sodium.

Serve Cornmeal Bacon Shortcakes with Lower Salt Cheese Sauce (page 13), if desired. For more zip, add one teaspoon finely chopped jalapeño pepper to shortcake batter.

HAM & CHEESE ROLLS

Makes 8 rolls

1 (16½-ounce) can
  boysenberries,* drained
  and juice reserved
2 tablespoons cornstarch
1 teaspoon sugar
3 ounces Armour Lower Salt
  Monterey Jack Cheese, cut
  into 8 (2½×¼-inch) strips
8 slices (1 ounce each) Armour
  Lower Salt Ham

To make boysenberry sauce, combine reserved boysenberry juice, cornstarch and sugar in small saucepan. Mix well to dissolve cornstarch. Cook over medium heat until mixture comes to a boil, stirring frequently. Cook for 1 minute. Fold in boysenberries; keep warm.

Preheat oven to 350°F. Place 1 cheese strip at narrow end of each ham slice; top with 1 tablespoon boysenberry sauce. Roll up; secure with wooden toothpicks, if needed. Place in single layer in ungreased 9×9-inch pan. Bake about 5 to 7 minutes, or until cheese is softened. Serve with remaining warm boysenberry sauce.

*If canned boysenberries are not available, substitute an equal amount of your favorite canned berries.

MICROWAVE DIRECTIONS:
Combine reserved juice, cornstarch and sugar in large microwave-safe dish. Mix well to dissolve cornstarch. Fold in boysenberries. Cover with vented plastic wrap; cook on Medium-High power (70%) about 3 to 6 minutes, or until thickened. Assemble ham rolls as directed above, placing them in 9×9-inch microwave-safe casserole dish. Cook, covered, on Medium power (50%) about 3 to 4 minutes, or until cheese is softened. Serve with remaining warm boysenberry sauce.

NUTRITION INFORMATION PER ROLL:
149 calories, 8.4 g protein, 4.9 g fat, 17.6 g carbohydrates, 25.2 mg cholesterol, 283 mg sodium.

LOWER SALT CHEESE SAUCE

Makes about 1⅔ cups

2 tablespoons unsalted margarine or butter
2 tablespoons all-purpose flour
1⅔ cups skim milk
1 to 2 teaspoons Mrs. Dash®, original blend
1 cup (4 ounces) shredded Armour Lower Salt Cheddar Cheese

Melt margarine in medium saucepan over medium heat. Stir in flour to make a paste. Gradually stir in milk, then seasoning. Bring to boil, stirring constantly. Cook for 5 minutes, or until sauce thickens. Stir in cheese until melted. Pour into blender or food processor container; process until smooth.

MICROWAVE DIRECTIONS:
Place margarine in large microwave-safe bowl or casserole dish. Cook on High power for 1 minute. Stir in flour to make a paste. Gradually stir in milk, then seasoning. Cover with vented plastic wrap; cook on High power about 4 to 6 minutes, or until thickened, stirring twice during cooking. Stir in cheese. Cook on High power about 30 seconds to 1 minute, or until cheese is melted. Pour into blender or food processor container; process until smooth.

VARIATIONS:
Stir 1 teaspoon finely chopped jalapeño peppers into cheese sauce.

Stir 1 tablespoon finely chopped red pepper into cheese sauce.

NUTRITION INFORMATION PER ¼ CUP:
125 calories, 5.9 g protein, 10.1 g fat, 3.9 g carbohydrates, 20.5 mg cholesterol, 85 mg sodium.

For a tasty treat, add five slices crisp, crumbled Armour Lower Salt Bacon to Lower Salt Cheese Sauce.

TROPICAL SALAD IN PINEAPPLE BOATS

Makes 4 servings

1 fresh pineapple
1½ cups (6 ounces) Armour
    Lower Salt Ham cut into
    julienne strips
1 cup fresh sweet cherries,
    pitted *or* canned sweet
    cherries, well drained
1 cup seedless red or green
    grapes, cut in half
2 oranges, peeled and
    sectioned
1 cup sliced celery
½ cup chopped unsalted
    cashews
¾ cup bottled low sodium, low
    calorie sweet & spicy salad
    dressing

Cut pineapple lengthwise into
quarters; remove core. Cut out
flesh; reserve shells. Cut flesh into
1-inch chunks. Combine
pineapple chunks and remaining
ingredients in large bowl; blend
well. Cover; refrigerate at least 1
hour before serving. Spoon evenly
into reserved pineapple shells.
Garnish with fresh sage, if
desired.

NUTRITION INFORMATION PER SERVING:
385 calories, 13.3 g protein, 10.5 g fat,
64.6 g carbohydrates, 21 mg cholesterol,
406 mg sodium.

FRUIT & HAM KABOBS

Makes 8 to 10 kabobs

2 tablespoons unsalted
    margarine or butter
¾ cup pineapple juice
¼ cup packed brown sugar
1 Armour Lower Salt Ham
    Nugget (about 1¾ pounds),
    cut into 1¼-inch cubes
2 large red apples, cored and
    cut into sixths
2 large green apples, cored and
    cut into sixths
1 fresh pineapple, peeled,
    cored and cut into 1-inch
    chunks
3 kiwifruit, peeled and cut
    into ½-inch slices

Preheat oven to 350°F. Place
margarine, pineapple juice and
brown sugar in bottom of large
casserole dish. Heat in oven until
margarine is melted. Thread ham,
apples, pineapple and kiwifruit
onto 8 to 10 (10-inch) metal or
wooden skewers, alternating the
ingredients. Place kabobs in hot
sauce; turn to coat all sides with
sauce. Bake about 20 to 25
minutes, or until heated through.
Turn kabobs twice during
cooking, basting with sauce
mixture. Serve over rice and
garnish with red grapes, if
desired.

NUTRITION INFORMATION PER KABOB:
277 calories, 15.1 g protein, 6.8 g fat,
37.2 g carbohydrates, 39.2 mg
cholesterol, 676 mg sodium.

Fruit & Ham Kabobs

PUFF PASTRY PIZZA

Makes 6 servings

1/2 (17¼-ounce) package frozen
    puff pastry (1 sheet)
8 ounces light cream cheese,
    softened
¼ cup sliced green onions
4 to 6 teaspoons skim milk
2 cups mixed salad greens,
    washed and drained
3 ounces Armour Lower Salt
    Ham, cut into 6 thin slices
½ medium avocado, peeled,
    pitted and cut into 6 slices
1 small tomato, cut into
    6 wedges
2 tablespoons bottled low
    sodium, low calorie
    creamy Italian salad
    dressing

Preheat oven to 375°F. Thaw pastry according to package directions. Roll pastry to 12-inch square on lightly floured surface; cut into 12-inch circle. Place on large cookie sheet or pizza pan. Generously prick bottom with fork, making sure pricks go all the way through dough. Bake about 10 to 12 minutes, or until golden brown. Cool in pan.

Combine cream cheese with green onions in small bowl; thin with enough milk to make spreading consistency. Gently spread cream cheese mixture over pastry leaving a 1-inch border. Top with salad greens. Roll up ham slices and place spoke-fashion on top of greens. Arrange avocado slices and tomato wedges between ham rolls. Drizzle with salad dressing. If desired, sprinkle pizza with 1 ounce shredded lower salt Monterey Jack cheese and broil 6 inches from heat source about 1 to 2 minutes, or until cheese is melted. Garnish with green onion flower in center of pizza, if desired. Cut into 6 wedges. Serve immediately.

NUTRITION INFORMATION PER SERVING: 344 calories, 9.8 g protein, 24.5 g fat, 19.7 g carbohydrates, 40.5 mg cholesterol, 481 mg sodium.

◆◆◆

For added flavor, top Puff Pastry Pizza with four slices crisp, crumbled Armour Lower Salt Bacon.

Puff Pastry Pizza

LUNCHEON FARE

LOAF SANDWICHES WITH BACON & HAM

Makes 6 servings

1/4 cup unsalted margarine or
  butter, melted
1 to 2 teaspoons garlic powder
1 large loaf French bread
3 ounces Armour Lower Salt
  Ham, thinly sliced
2 ounces Armour Lower Salt
  Monterey Jack Cheese,
  thinly sliced
6 cherry tomato slices
6 slices Armour Lower Salt
  Bacon, cut in half and
  cooked crisp
12 (1/4-inch) zucchini slices

Combine margarine and garlic powder in small bowl; set aside. Make 6 diagonal cuts at equal distances along loaf of bread, cutting 3/4 of the way through loaf. Spread margarine mixture on cut sides of bread. Evenly distribute ham and cheese among cuts. Place 1 tomato slice, 2 bacon pieces and 2 zucchini slices in each cut. If desired, wrap entire loaf with foil and bake in 375°F. oven about 15 to 20 minutes, or until cheese is melted. Cut into 6 servings.

NUTRITION INFORMATION PER SERVING: 380 calories, 14.1 g protein, 16.3 g fat, 44 g carbohydrates, 23 mg cholesterol, 701 mg sodium.

SPINACH SALAD WITH RASPBERRY DRESSING

Makes 2 servings

½ cup plain nonfat yogurt
¼ cup fresh or frozen red
    raspberries, thawed if
    frozen
1 tablespoon skim milk
1½ teaspoons chopped fresh
    mint *or* ½ teaspoon dried
    mint, crushed
4 to 6 cups fresh spinach,
    washed, drained and
    trimmed
2 large fresh mushrooms,
    sliced
1 tablespoon sesame seeds,
    toasted
4 to 6 red onion rings
6 slices Armour Lower Salt
    Bacon, cooked crisp and
    crumbled

Carefully combine yogurt, raspberries, milk and mint in small bowl; set aside. Combine spinach, mushrooms and sesame seeds in medium bowl; mix well. Arrange spinach mixture evenly on 2 individual salad plates; top with red onion rings. Drizzle yogurt dressing over salads; sprinkle with bacon. Garnish with fresh raspberries and mint sprig, if desired.

NUTRITION INFORMATION PER SERVING:
200 calories, 15.8 g protein, 10.1 g fat, 14.1 g carbohydrates, 19.1 mg cholesterol, 556 mg sodium.

CITRUS, AVOCADO & BACON SALAD

Makes 2 servings

3 tablespoons orange juice
    concentrate, thawed
2 tablespoons vegetable oil
1 tablespoon lime juice
1 tablespoon honey
1 tablespoon white vinegar
3 cups mixed salad greens,
    washed and drained
½ avocado, peeled, pitted and
    sliced
6 slices Armour Lower Salt
    Bacon, cut in half and
    cooked crisp
1 (11-ounce) can mandarin
    oranges, drained

Combine orange juice concentrate, oil, lime juice, honey and vinegar in small bowl; set aside. Divide mixed salad greens evenly between 2 individual salad plates. Arrange avocado and bacon spoke-fashion over greens. Arrange mandarin oranges on top of greens. Drizzle with dressing. Garnish with chopped unsalted peanuts, if desired.

NUTRITION INFORMATION PER SERVING:
496 calories, 9.4 g protein, 30.6 g fat, 51.5 g carbohydrates, 18 mg cholesterol, 398 mg sodium.

Top: Spinach Salad with Raspberry Dressing; bottom: Citrus, Avocado & Bacon Salad

Look for sun-ripened, no salt added, dried tomatoes in the specialty produce section of your local supermarket.

SUN-DRIED TOMATO & CHEESE TART

Makes 6 servings

3/4 cup sun-ripened, no salt
    added, dried tomatoes
1 (9-inch) refrigerated
    unbaked pie crust
1 cup (4 ounces) shredded
    Armour Lower Salt
    Cheddar Cheese
1 1/2 cups (6 ounces) Armour
    Lower Salt Ham cut into
    1/4-inch cubes
3 tablespoons chopped fresh
    basil *or* 1 tablespoon dried
    basil
1/2 teaspoon Mrs. Dash®,
    original blend

Preheat oven to 425°F. Blanch dried tomatoes by placing in boiling water for 2 minutes before using; drain. Cut into thirds.

Press pie crust into 9-inch tart pan; press firmly against side and bottom. Prick crust generously with fork. Bake for 7 minutes. *Reduce oven temperature to 375°F.* Sprinkle crust with half the cheese; top with ham and seasonings. Arrange tomatoes over top in single layer. Top with remaining cheese. Bake about 7 to 9 minutes, or until cheese is

melted and crust is lightly browned. Let stand 5 minutes before serving. Cut into 6 wedges. Garnish with fresh basil sprigs, if desired.

NUTRITION INFORMATION PER SERVING: 308 calories, 12.8 g protein, 17.6 g fat, 24.6 g carbohydrates, 34 mg cholesterol, 454 mg sodium.

HAWAIIAN-STYLE SALAD

Makes 4 servings

2 cups (8 ounces) Armour
    Lower Salt Ham cut into
    1-inch cubes
1 (15 1/4-ounce) can pineapple
    chunks, drained
1 cup thinly sliced celery
1/4 cup slivered almonds,
    toasted
1 cup plain nonfat yogurt
    Leaf lettuce, washed and
    drained
1/4 cup shredded coconut,
    toasted

Combine ham, pineapple, celery, almonds and yogurt in medium bowl. Cover; refrigerate at least 1 hour before serving to blend flavors. To serve, arrange ham mixture on lettuce-lined tray or platter. Sprinkle with coconut.

NUTRITION INFORMATION PER SERVING: 258 calories, 15.3 g protein, 8.4 g fat, 28 g carbohydrates, 29 mg cholesterol, 566 mg sodium.

HAM-FILLED POTATO BOATS

Makes 4 servings

1⅓ cups instant mashed potato
　　granules
2 tablespoons unsalted
　　margarine or butter
⅓ cup skim milk
1 egg, slightly beaten
½ (10½-ounce) can white sauce
1 cup (4 ounces) Armour
　　Lower Salt Ham cut into
　　½-inch cubes
⅔ cup drained canned corn
　　with red and green sweet
　　peppers
½ cup (2 ounces) shredded
　　Armour Lower Salt Colby
　　Cheese

Preheat oven to 400°F. Prepare
instant potatoes according to
package directions for 4 servings,
using 1⅓ cups water, unsalted
margarine and skim milk,
omitting salt. Add egg to potato
mixture. Add additional potato
granules or water, if needed, so
mixture holds its shape. Spray
baking sheet with nonstick
cooking spray. Spoon potato
mixture equally into 4 mounds
onto baking sheet. Make
indentation in center of each
mound with back of large spoon.
Bake about 13 to 15 minutes, or
until potatoes are light brown.

Meanwhile, heat white sauce in
small saucepan over medium heat
until warm. Add ham and corn;
heat until ham is hot. Spoon corn
mixture evenly into baked potato

boats; sprinkle with cheese. Heat
in 400°F. oven about 2 to 3
minutes, or until cheese is melted.

NUTRITION INFORMATION PER SERVING:
322 calories, 13.5 g protein, 17.2 g fat,
27.5 g carbohydrates, 97.6 mg
cholesterol, 594 mg sodium.

ZESTY PASTA SALAD

Makes 4 to 6 servings

2 cups (8 ounces) Armour
　　Lower Salt Ham cut into
　　julienne strips
2 cups uncooked pasta bowties
　　or shells, cooked according
　　to package directions
　　omitting salt and drained
8 ounces California-blend
　　frozen vegetables, thawed
5 cherry tomatoes, cut in half
¾ cup bottled low sodium,
　　reduced calorie zesty
　　Italian salad dressing
　　Mixed greens, washed and
　　drained

Combine ham, pasta, vegetables,
tomatoes and salad dressing in
large bowl; toss to coat well.
Cover; refrigerate at least 1 hour
before serving to blend flavors. To
serve, arrange pasta mixture in
lettuce-lined bowl or on platter.
Garnish with red and green
pepper rings, if desired.

NUTRITION INFORMATION PER SERVING:
233 calories, 12.3 g protein, 2.6 g fat,
38 g carbohydrates, 18.6 mg cholesterol,
344 mg sodium.

Zesty Pasta Salad

CARIBBEAN BANANA & HAM SALAD

Makes 4 to 6 servings

3 green (unripe) bananas,
    peeled
2 cups (8 ounces) Armour
    Lower Salt Ham cut into
    ½-inch cubes
2 medium carrots, shredded
1 small cucumber, sliced
1 medium tomato, chopped
1 medium avocado, peeled,
    pitted and cut into cubes
1 stalk celery, sliced
⅔ cup bottled low calorie, low
    sodium red wine vinegar
    salad dressing

Heat bananas in 2 cups water in
large skillet over medium-high
heat to boiling. Reduce heat; cover
and simmer about 3 to 5 minutes,
or until bananas are tender. Drain
and cool. Cut bananas crosswise
into ½-inch slices.

Combine banana slices and
remaining ingredients in large
bowl. Toss gently to coat well.
Cover; refrigerate at least 1 hour
before serving to blend flavors.
Serve on leaf lettuce and garnish
with carrot curls, if desired.

NUTRITION INFORMATION PER SERVING:
191 calories, 8.6 g protein, 8.1 g fat,
20.5 g carbohydrates, 18.6 mg
cholesterol, 359 mg sodium.

*Caribbean Banana & Ham Salad
offers a unique way to use green
(unripe) bananas. If bananas are
difficult to peel, make a shallow,
lengthwise cut along natural ridge
of fruit; pull peel off in sections.*

AVOCADO & BACON PITAS

Makes 4 sandwiches

2 (6-inch) pita breads, cut in
    half
4 leaves leaf lettuce, washed
    and drained
12 slices Armour Lower Salt
    Bacon, cut in half and
    cooked crisp
1 avocado, peeled, pitted and
    sliced
1 (15¼-ounce) can pineapple
    spears, well drained
4 radishes, thinly sliced
8 tablespoons bottled low
    sodium, reduced calorie
    zesty Italian salad
    dressing

Open sliced edges of pita bread
halves. Line with leaf lettuce.
Divide bacon, avocado, pineapple
and radishes evenly among bread
pockets. Before serving, spoon 2
tablespoons of the dressing over
top of each sandwich.

*NUTRITION INFORMATION PER
SANDWICH:* 319 calories, 10.1 g protein,
17.2 g fat, 35.2 g carbohydrates, 18 mg
cholesterol, 558 mg sodium.

BACON TIMBALE

Makes 6 servings

3 tablespoons unsalted
  margarine or butter
1 small onion, finely chopped
2 tablespoons all-purpose
  flour
2 cups evaporated skim milk,
  divided
4 eggs, beaten
1 teaspoon no salt added
  chicken flavor instant
  bouillon
6 slices Armour Lower Salt
  Bacon, cut into thirds and
  cooked crisp
½ cup chopped fresh spinach,
  washed and drained
  Boiling water

Preheat oven to 350°F. Melt margarine in large skillet over medium heat. Add onion; sauté about 3 to 5 minutes, or until soft. Stir in flour until well blended; cook 1 minute, stirring frequently. Gradually stir in 1 cup evaporated milk. Cook, stirring frequently, until mixture thickens slightly. Remove from heat; set aside.

Combine eggs, bouillon and remaining 1 cup evaporated milk in medium bowl. Stir in onion mixture, bacon and spinach. Spray 8×8-inch casserole dish with nonstick cooking spray; pour in bacon mixture. Set dish in 13×9-inch pan; place on oven rack. Pour boiling water into pan to come halfway up sides of dish. Bake for 35 minutes, or until knife inserted into center comes out clean. Let stand 5 minutes before serving. Garnish with parsley, if desired.

MICROWAVE DIRECTIONS:
Place margarine in small microwave-safe bowl. Cook on High power for 1 minute; add onion. Cover with vented plastic wrap; cook on High power for 2 minutes. Stir in flour until well blended. Gradually stir in 1 cup evaporated milk. Cook, covered, on Medium-High power (70%) for 3 minutes; set aside. Combine eggs, bouillon and remaining 1 cup evaporated milk in medium bowl. Stir in onion mixture, bacon and spinach. Spray 10-inch microwave-safe tube pan with nonstick cooking spray; pour in bacon mixture. Set tube pan in larger microwave-safe casserole dish; place in microwave oven. Pour boiling water into dish to come halfway up side of tube pan. Cook, uncovered, on Medium-High power (70%) about 18 to 20 minutes, or until knife inserted near center comes out clean. Let stand 5 minutes before serving. Garnish as above.

NUTRITION INFORMATION PER SERVING: 219 calories, 12.6 g protein, 12.6 g fat, 13.6 g carbohydrates, 192 mg cholesterol, 276 mg sodium.

For added flavor, serve Bacon Timbale with Lower Salt Cheese Sauce (page 13).

FRUITED HAM SAUCE OVER SHORTCAKES

Makes 6 servings

1 (13-ounce) package apple
    cinnamon muffin mix
1 egg
    Skim milk
1½ cups (6 ounces) Armour
    Lower Salt Ham cut into
    ¼-inch cubes
1 cup canned lite apple fruit
    filling
¼ cup raisins
1 orange, peel grated and
    orange sectioned

Preheat oven to 400°F. Spray 6 shortcake cups or 3 Texas-size muffin tin cups with nonstick cooking spray. Prepare muffin mix according to package directions, using egg and skim milk. Divide batter evenly among prepared cups. Bake about 15 to 25 minutes, or until golden brown. Remove from pan to wire rack; set aside.

Meanwhile, heat ham, apple fruit filling, raisins and orange peel and sections in medium saucepan over medium heat about 7 to 9 minutes, or until hot and bubbly.

Place shortcakes or halved Texas-size muffins on individual serving plates; spoon ham and fruit mixture over top. Garnish with fresh mint, if desired.

MICROWAVE DIRECTIONS:
Prepare shortcakes as directed above. Combine ham, apple fruit filling, raisins and orange peel and sections in large microwave-safe bowl. Cover with vented plastic wrap; cook on High power about 4 to 6 minutes, or until sauce is hot and bubbly. Assemble shortcakes as directed above. Garnish as above.

NUTRITION INFORMATION PER SERVING: 318 calories, 9.6 g protein, 8.9 g fat, 49.5 g carbohydrates, 60 mg cholesterol, 529 mg sodium.

◆◆◆

Look for shortcake or Texas-size muffin tins in specialty food stores or in the housewares department of large retail stores.

TOASTED APPLE & HAM SANDWICHES

Makes 2 servings

2 large slices sourdough
    bread, toasted
4 tablespoons apple,
    cinnamon, wheat, raisin
    and walnut yogurt
4 ounces Armour Lower Salt
    Ham, thinly sliced
¼ cup (1 ounce) shredded
    Armour Lower Salt
    Monterey Jack Cheese

Spread 1 side of each toast slice with 2 tablespoons yogurt. Cover each with 2 ounces ham; sprinkle with cheese. Broil 4 to 6 inches from heat source or in toaster oven about 3 to 5 minutes, or until cheese is melted. Garnish with apple slice and parsley, if desired.

NUTRITION INFORMATION PER SERVING: 251 calories, 17.7 g protein, 7.9 g fat, 8.4 g carbohydrates, 44.2 mg cholesterol, 732 mg sodium.

Fruited Ham Sauce over Shortcakes

CALIFORNIA-STYLE TOSTADAS

Makes 8 tostadas

Vegetable oil
8 (6-inch) corn tortillas
4 cups mixed salad greens,
    washed and drained
8 slices Armour Lower Salt
    Bacon, cut into fourths and
    cooked crisp
1 medium tomato, chopped
4 green onions, sliced
1 medium avocado, peeled,
    pitted and cut into cubes
½ cup (2 ounces) shredded
    Armour Lower Salt
    Cheddar Cheese

Heat ¼ inch oil in large skillet
over medium heat until hot. Fry 1
tortilla at a time in oil for 30
seconds on each side, or until
crisp and light brown; drain on
paper towels. Keep warm in
200°F. oven no longer than 20
minutes. Arrange about ½ cup of
the salad greens on top of each
tortilla. Top each with 4 bacon
pieces, tomato, green onions and
avocado; sprinkle with cheese.
Garnish with cilantro and serve
with salsa, if desired.

NUTRITION INFORMATION PER TOSTADA:
162 calories, 6 g protein, 11.5 g fat, 10.8 g
carbohydrates, 13.5 mg cholesterol,
231 mg sodium.

LAYERED VEGETABLE & MEAT SALAD

Makes 6 to 8 servings

4 cups salad greens, washed
    and drained
2 large carrots, shredded
3 medium zucchini, shredded
4 cups (16 ounces) shredded
    Armour Lower Salt Ham
3 cups sliced cauliflowerets
1½ cups (6 ounces) shredded
    Armour Lower Salt
    Cheddar Cheese
8 slices Armour Lower Salt
    Bacon, cooked crisp and
    crumbled
8 ounces bottled low sodium,
    reduced calorie zesty
    Italian salad dressing

Spread half the salad greens
evenly along bottom of large glass
salad bowl. Layer carrots,
zucchini, ham and cauliflower
over salad greens. Top with
remaining greens. Sprinkle with
cheese, then bacon. Before
serving, drizzle top of salad with
dressing. Garnish with fresh sage,
if desired.

NUTRITION INFORMATION PER SERVING:
234 calories, 19.6 g protein, 12.1 g fat,
10.3 g carbohydrates, 56.5 mg
cholesterol, 722 mg sodium.

BACON PILAF

Makes 4 to 6 servings

2 tablespoons unsalted
  margarine or butter
2 medium tomatoes, coarsely
  chopped
¼ cup sliced green onions
8 slices Armour Lower Salt
  Bacon, cooked crisp and
  crumbled
1 cup uncooked rice
1 teaspoon no salt added
  chicken flavor instant
  bouillon

Melt margarine in large skillet or
saucepan over medium heat. Add
tomatoes and green onions; sauté
for 2 minutes. Stir in 2 cups water
and remaining ingredients. Heat
to boiling; reduce heat and cover.
Simmer about 20 to 25 minutes, or
until liquid is absorbed. Fluff rice
with fork before serving. Garnish
with parsley, if desired.

MICROWAVE DIRECTIONS:

Place margarine, tomatoes and
green onions in large microwave-
safe casserole dish. Cook, covered,
on High power for 5 minutes. Add
2 cups water and remaining
ingredients; cover. Cook on High
power for 5 minutes. Reduce
power to Medium-High (70%);
cook about 10 to 12 minutes, or
until liquid is absorbed. Let stand,
covered, 5 minutes. Fluff rice with
fork before serving. Garnish as
above.

NUTRITION INFORMATION PER SERVING:
197 calories, 5.3 g protein, 7.6 g fat,
27.2 g carbohydrates, 8.2 mg cholesterol,
175 mg sodium.

EAST INDIAN PEACH SALAD

Makes 4 servings

½ cup vanilla lowfat yogurt
½ teaspoon curry powder, or to
  taste
1 (16-ounce) can sliced peaches
  in light syrup, drained
  and syrup reserved
2 cups (8 ounces) Armour
  Lower Salt Ham cut into
  ½-inch cubes
1 cup seedless red or green
  grapes, cut in half
  Leaf lettuce, washed and
  drained
2 tablespoons sliced almonds,
  toasted

Combine yogurt, curry powder
and 1 tablespoon reserved peach
syrup in small bowl; set aside.
Combine peaches, ham and
grapes in medium bowl. Add
yogurt mixture; toss gently to coat
well. Serve in lettuce-lined
serving bowl or platter. Sprinkle
with almonds.

NUTRITION INFORMATION PER SERVING:
206 calories, 12.3 g protein, 5.1 g fat,
25.7 g carbohydrates, 29.2 mg
cholesterol, 509 mg sodium.

MAIN MEAL DISHES

PINEAPPLE-ORANGE GLAZED HAM

Makes 8 to 10 servings

1 Armour Lower Salt Ham Nugget (about 1¾ pounds)
⅔ cup orange marmalade
1 (8-ounce) can pineapple chunks, drained and juice reserved

Preheat oven to 350°F. Spray roasting pan with nonstick cooking spray; place ham in pan. Combine orange marmalade, 2 tablespoons reserved pineapple juice and pineapple chunks in small bowl. Spoon a third over ham; brush to cover entire surface. Bake, uncovered, for 1 hour and 10 minutes, or until ham reaches an internal temperature of 145°F. Baste with pineapple-marmalade sauce every 10 minutes. Serve with remaining sauce. Garnish with fresh mint leaves or parsley, if desired.

NUTRITION INFORMATION PER SERVING: 185 calories, 14.1 g protein, 3.9 g fat, 17.2 g carbohydrates, 39.2 mg cholesterol, 672 mg sodium.

Try apricot-pineapple jam in place of orange marmalade in Pineapple-Orange Glazed Ham for a different flavor combination.

CHUNKY HAM STEW

Makes 4 to 6 servings

1 medium onion, chopped
2 stalks celery, sliced
2 carrots, sliced
4 cups low sodium chicken
  broth
2 cups (8 ounces) Armour
  Lower Salt Ham cut into
  $1/2$-inch cubes
1 tablespoon Mrs. Dash®,
  original blend
1 cup frozen peas
2 tablespoons cornstarch

Combine onion, celery, carrots, broth, ham and seasoning in Dutch oven. Cover and cook over medium-high heat for 20 minutes, or until carrots are almost tender. Stir in peas. Mix $1/4$ cup water and cornstarch; add to stew, stirring constantly until thickened. If desired, garnish with celery leaves and serve with Bacon Dumplings (recipe on page 38).

MICROWAVE DIRECTIONS:
Combine ingredients as directed above in 10-inch microwave-safe tube pan. Cover with vented plastic wrap. Cook on High power for 10 minutes. Stir; rotate pan. Continue cooking, covered, on High power about 10 to 15 minutes, or until carrots are almost tender. Stir in peas. Mix $1/4$ cup water and cornstarch; stir into stew. Cook, covered, on High power about 2 to 3 minutes, or until thickened, stirring 3 times

during cooking. Garnish as above. If desired, serve with Bacon Dumplings (recipe on page 38).

NUTRITION INFORMATION PER SERVING:
131 calories, 10.6 g protein, 3.4 g fat, 12.6 g carbohydrates, 19.2 mg cholesterol, 410 mg sodium.

POTATO-LEEK SOUP

Makes 6 servings

2 tablespoons unsalted
  margarine or butter
1 cup sliced leeks
2 green onions, sliced
4 medium potatoes, peeled
  and cut into cubes
1 cup (4 ounces) Armour
  Lower Salt Ham cut into
  $1/2$-inch cubes
$1^1/2$ tablespoons chicken flavor
  no salt added instant
  bouillon
$1/2$ tablespoon Mrs. Dash®,
  original blend

Melt margarine in Dutch oven over medium heat. Add leeks and green onions; sauté until tender. Add remaining ingredients and 5 cups water. Bring to boil over medium-high heat. Reduce heat to simmer. Cook, uncovered, about 30 to 40 minutes, or until potatoes are tender. Season with freshly ground pepper, if desired.

NUTRITION INFORMATION PER SERVING:
162 calories, 5.2 g protein, 5.8 g fat, 22.1 g carbohydrates, 10 mg cholesterol, 171 mg sodium.

Top: Bacon Dumplings (page 38); bottom: Chunky Ham Stew

BACON DUMPLINGS

Makes 8 to 12 servings

1 (12-ounce) package Armour
    Lower Salt Bacon
3 cups skim milk
1 cup couscous or enriched
    farina hot cereal
¼ cup finely chopped onions
2 eggs, well beaten
1 tablespoon unsalted
    margarine or butter
    Pepper to taste
¼ cup unsalted margarine or
    butter
¾ cup (3 ounces) shredded
    Armour Lower Salt
    Monterey Jack Cheese

Cook bacon slices until crisp; crumble and set aside. Heat milk to approximately 208°F. in large saucepan over medium heat. Add couscous; stir constantly, cooking until very thick. Stir in bacon and onions. Add eggs, 1 tablespoon margarine and pepper, stirring well. Spray 13×9-inch pan with nonstick cooking spray; spread couscous mixture in pan. Cover and cool in refrigerator until firm, for 2 hours, or place in freezer about 20 to 30 minutes.

Preheat oven to 350°F. Cut firm dumpling mixture into 1½-inch circles or squares, dipping cutter into cold water to prevent sticking. Overlap dumplings in ungreased round baking dish or ovenproof skillet. Melt ¼ cup margarine; drizzle over dumplings. Top with cheese. Bake for 30 minutes, or until golden brown and crisp. If desired, serve dumplings on top of Chunky Ham Stew (recipe on page 36) or serve as an appetizer.

NUTRITION INFORMATION PER SERVING: 200 calories, 9.8 g protein, 12 g fat, 14.1 g carbohydrates, 63.4 mg cholesterol, 262 mg sodium.

HAM FRIED RICE

Makes 6 servings

4 tablespoons peanut oil,
    divided
4 green onions, chopped
1 small red pepper, cut into
    strips
5 medium-size fresh
    mushrooms, sliced
1 cup frozen peas
1 (8-ounce) can sliced water
    chestnuts, drained
3 cups cooked instant rice
2½ cups (10 ounces) Armour
    Lower Salt Ham cut into
    julienne strips

Heat 2 tablespoons of the oil in wok or large skillet over high heat. Add green onions and red pepper; sauté for 2 minutes, or until tender-crisp. Add remaining 2 tablespoons oil to wok and heat. Add mushrooms and peas; sauté until peas are tender-crisp. Add water chestnuts, rice and ham. Cook over medium heat until mixture is hot, stirring frequently. If desired, add 2 tablespoons dry white wine for additional flavor and garnish with red and green pepper rings.

NUTRITION INFORMATION PER SERVING: 275 calories, 12.6 g protein, 11.8 g fat, 27.6 g carbohydrates, 23.2 mg cholesterol, 435 mg sodium.

STUFFED BAKED POTATOES

Makes 4 servings

1 (12-ounce) package Armour
 Lower Salt Bacon
4 large baking potatoes
1 tablespoon vegetable oil
4 medium-size fresh
 mushrooms, sliced
1 (8-ounce) carton plain nonfat
 yogurt
¼ cup dairy sour cream
2 tablespoons snipped fresh
 chives

Preheat oven to 400°F. Cook
bacon slices until crisp; crumble
and set aside. Prick potatoes with
fork several times; place on baking
sheet. Bake for 1 hour, or until
fork tender. Heat oil in small
skillet over medium heat. Add
mushrooms. Sauté until almost
tender; keep warm.

Combine yogurt, sour cream and
chives in small bowl; mix well.
Cut potatoes lengthwise in half;
fluff center with fork, making an
indentation to hold sauce. Spoon
an eighth of the yogurt sauce
evenly onto each potato half.
Divide bacon and mushrooms
evenly over tops of potatoes.
Garnish with parsley and freshly
ground pepper, if desired.

NUTRITION INFORMATION PER SERVING:
448 calories, 18.1 g protein, 17.6 g fat,
55.7 g carbohydrates, 34.2 mg
cholesterol, 632 mg sodium.

HAM PASTA PRIMAVERA

Makes 4 to 6 servings

3 tablespoons unsalted
 margarine or butter,
 divided
1 cup pea pods
½ cup shredded carrots
3 green onions, sliced
1 small red pepper, cut into
 strips
¾ cup evaporated skim milk
3 cups (12 ounces) Armour
 Lower Salt Ham cut into
 small cubes
10 ounces uncooked spaghetti,
 cooked according to
 package directions
 omitting salt and drained

Melt 1 tablespoon of the
margarine in medium skillet over
medium heat. Add vegetables;
sauté until tender. Add remaining
2 tablespoons margarine, milk
and ham. Cook over medium-
high heat about 3 to 4 minutes, or
until mixture thickens slightly.
Serve over warm spaghetti.
Garnish with fresh basil, cilantro
or freshly ground pepper, if
desired.

NUTRITION INFORMATION PER SERVING:
347 calories, 19 g protein, 9.7 g fat,
43.5 g carbohydrates, 29.1 mg
cholesterol, 521 mg sodium.

*Reduce calories in Ham Pasta
Primavera by substituting nonstick
cooking spray for margarine when
sautéing vegetables.*

HOT DOG CHILI

Makes 6 servings

1 tablespoon vegetable oil
1 medium onion, coarsely chopped
1 small green pepper, coarsely chopped
2 cloves garlic, finely chopped
2 (8-ounce) cans no salt added tomato sauce
1½ tablespoons chili powder
1 (15-ounce) can red kidney beans, undrained
8 Armour Lower Salt Jumbo Beef Hot Dogs, cut into fourths

Heat oil in Dutch oven over medium heat until hot. Add onion, green pepper and garlic; sauté until tender. Add tomato sauce and chili powder; simmer, uncovered, for 10 minutes. Add undrained beans and hot dog chunks; simmer until heated through. Serve with low salt crackers, if desired.

MICROWAVE DIRECTIONS:
Omit oil. Place onion, green pepper and garlic in large microwave-safe casserole dish. Cook, covered, on High power about 4 to 5 minutes, or until onion and pepper are tender. Add tomato sauce, chili powder and undrained beans; cook, covered, on High power for 5 minutes. Stir in hot dog chunks. Cook, covered, on High power about 4 to 6 minutes, or until hot dogs are heated through and flavor has developed.

NUTRITION INFORMATION PER SERVING:
359 calories, 15.6 g protein, 23 g fat, 24.6 g carbohydrates, 40 mg cholesterol, 632 mg sodium.

Prepare Hot Dog Chili ahead of time and refrigerate until ready to heat and serve. It also makes a great filling for a hot sandwich.

CREAMY SPINACH FETTUCINI

Makes 4 to 6 servings

1 small green pepper, chopped
1 small red pepper, chopped
1 small onion, chopped
1 (8-ounce) carton plain nonfat yogurt
½ cup canned white sauce
2 tablespoons dried Italian seasoning
1½ cups (6 ounces) Armour Lower Salt Ham cut into ½-inch cubes
12 ounces uncooked spinach fettucini, cooked according to package directions omitting salt and drained
6 slices Armour Lower Salt Bacon, cooked crisp and crumbled

Spray large skillet with nonstick cooking spray; place over medium heat. Add vegetables; sauté until tender-crisp. Mix yogurt, white sauce and seasoning in small bowl. Add to vegetables and heat through. Add ham; continue cooking until hot. Spoon over warm fettucini; top with bacon. Garnish with parsley or fresh rosemary, if desired.

NUTRITION INFORMATION PER SERVING:
352 calories, 17.7 g protein, 9 g fat, 48 g carbohydrates, 20.6 mg cholesterol, 531 mg sodium.

Hot Dog Chili

SPINACH-STUFFED HAM ROLLS

Makes 18 rolls

1½ **cups cooked rice**
  2 **green onions, sliced**
  1 **cup chopped fresh spinach, washed and drained**
 ¼ **teaspoon pepper**
27 **ounces Armour Lower Salt Ham, cut into 18 (1½-ounce) slices**
  1 **(20-ounce) can lite cherry fruit filling**
 ¼ **cup pecan halves**

Preheat oven to 350°F. Combine rice, green onions, spinach and pepper in medium bowl. Place 2 tablespoons rice mixture in center of each ham slice; roll up and secure with wooden toothpicks. Spray 13×9-inch baking pan with nonstick cooking spray; arrange ham rolls in pan. Bake, covered, for 30 minutes, or until heated through. Meanwhile, heat cherry fruit filling in small saucepan over medium heat until hot. Top ham rolls with hot cherry sauce; sprinkle with pecans.

MICROWAVE DIRECTIONS:
Assemble ham rolls as directed above. Spray 11×7½-inch microwave-safe dish with nonstick cooking spray; arrange ham rolls in dish. Cover with waxed paper. Cook on Medium-High power (70%) for 8 minutes. Top with cherry filling. Cook, uncovered, on High power about 2 to 4 minutes, or until sauce is hot; sprinkle with pecans.

NUTRITION INFORMATION PER ROLL:
195 calories, 13.8 g protein, 6.0 g fat, 19.2 g carbohydrates, 33.5 mg cholesterol, 590 mg sodium.

━━━━━━━━━━ ◆ ◆ ◆ ━━━━━━━━━━

Canned lite apple fruit filling also tastes great over the Spinach-Stuffed Ham Rolls.

SAVORY LENTIL SOUP

Makes 6 servings

1 **cup uncooked lentils**
3 **cups (12 ounces) Armour Lower Salt Ham cut into small cubes**
1 **(14½-ounce) can no salt added stewed tomatoes**
1 **small onion, chopped**
½ **cup chopped celery**
1 **teaspoon hot pepper sauce**
1 **teaspoon Mrs. Dash®, original blend**

Wash lentils; remove any grit or broken shells. Combine all ingredients in large covered kettle; stir in 4 cups water. Bring to boil over medium-high heat, stirring often. Reduce heat to simmer. Cover and cook for 1 hour, or until lentils are tender and soup is thick. Garnish with celery leaves, if desired.

NUTRITION INFORMATION PER SERVING:
220 calories, 19 g protein, 3.2 g fat, 26.7 g carbohydrates, 28 mg cholesterol, 537 mg sodium.

VEGETABLE AND HAM SOUP

Makes 6 to 8 servings

2 tablespoons unsalted
    margarine or butter
1 medium onion, coarsely
    chopped
2½ tablespoons no salt added
    chicken flavor instant
    bouillon
1 large potato, peeled and
    diced
1 (16-ounce) package frozen
    mixed vegetables
2½ cups (10 ounces) Armour
    Lower Salt Ham cut into
    ½-inch cubes
2 teaspoons Mrs. Dash®,
    original blend
    Pepper to taste

Melt margarine in Dutch oven
over medium heat. Add onion;
sauté until tender. Add remaining
ingredients and 5 cups water.
Bring to boil over medium-high
heat. Reduce heat to simmer.
Cook, uncovered, for 30 minutes,
or until potato is tender. Garnish
with carrot curls and fresh chives,
if desired.

MICROWAVE DIRECTIONS:

Place margarine and onion in 10-
inch microwave-safe tube pan.
Cover with vented plastic wrap;
cook on High power about 2 to 3
minutes, or until onion is tender.
Add remaining ingredients and 5
cups water. Cover with vented
plastic wrap. Cook on High power
for 10 minutes, or until boiling.
Reduce power to Medium-High
(70%); continue cooking for 30
minutes, or until potato is tender.
Garnish as above.

NUTRITION INFORMATION PER SERVING:
157 calories, 8.8 g protein, 5.7 g fat,
16.5 g carbohydrates, 18.2 mg
cholesterol, 334 mg sodium.

SPAGHETTI AND BACON TOSS

Makes 4 to 6 servings

4 green onions, chopped
1 small zucchini, sliced
½ cup canned white sauce
¼ cup skim milk
1 (8-ounce) carton plain nonfat
    yogurt
8 ounces uncooked spaghetti,
    cooked according to
    package directions
    omitting salt and drained
1 (12-ounce) package Armour
    Lower Salt Bacon, slices
    cooked crisp and crumbled
1 large fresh tomato, seeded
    and chopped

Spray medium saucepan with
nonstick cooking spray; place over
medium heat. Add green onions
and zucchini; sauté until tender.
Combine white sauce, milk and
yogurt in small bowl; add to
vegetables. Cook until heated
through and mixture steams. Toss
warm spaghetti with bacon; top
with sauce. Garnish each serving
with chopped tomato.

NUTRITION INFORMATION PER SERVING:
289 calories, 13.8 g protein, 10 g fat,
35.5 g carbohydrates, 18.7 mg
cholesterol, 485 mg sodium.

ARTICHOKE-STUFFED CHICKEN BREASTS

Makes 4 servings

4 boneless chicken breast
    halves, skinned
¼ cup finely chopped onion
10 slices Armour Lower Salt
    Bacon, cooked crisp and
    crumbled
1 (13¾-ounce) can artichoke
    hearts, well drained and
    chopped
1 teaspoon dill mustard
¼ cup unseasoned dry bread
    crumbs
1 teaspoon Mrs. Dash®,
    original blend
1 egg, slightly beaten

Preheat oven to 350°F. Pound chicken breasts to ¼-inch thickness; set aside. Combine onion, bacon, artichoke hearts and mustard in medium bowl. Spread a fourth of the artichoke mixture down center of each chicken breast. Roll up and fasten with wooden toothpicks. Place in single layer in ungreased baking dish. Mix bread crumbs and seasoning in small bowl; set aside. Brush rolled breasts with egg; sprinkle with seasoned crumbs. Bake about 30 to 35 minutes, or until chicken is done. If desired, drizzle with ¼ cup melted unsalted margarine or butter and broil about 2 to 3 minutes, or until lightly browned. Garnish with tomato wedges and fresh dill, if desired.

MICROWAVE DIRECTIONS:
Prepare chicken rolls as directed above. Spray 8×8-inch microwave-safe dish with nonstick cooking spray; place rolls in dish. Cover with waxed paper; cook on High power for 8 minutes. Rotate dish; continue cooking on High power about 6 to 8 minutes, or until chicken is almost done. Let stand, covered, about 2 to 4 minutes to finish cooking. Garnish as above.

NUTRITION INFORMATION PER SERVING: 291 calories, 36.2 g protein, 10.8 g fat, 11.3 g carbohydrates, 156 mg cholesterol, 486 mg sodium.

Artichoke-Stuffed Chicken Breasts is an elegant, yet easy, dish that is great to serve company.

APPLE-STUFFED HAM

Makes 8 to 10 servings

1 Armour Lower Salt Ham
    Nugget (about 1¾ pounds)
1 small red cooking apple,
    chopped
2 stalks celery, chopped
1 small onion, chopped
½ cup unseasoned dry bread
    crumbs
½ cup raisins
⅓ cup apple juice concentrate,
    thawed
2 teaspoons Mrs. Dash®,
    original blend
1 teaspoon ground cinnamon
    (optional)

Preheat oven to 375°F. Hollow out 3×2-inch opening in flat surface of ham. Finely chop ham scraps and mix with remaining ingredients in large bowl. Spoon enough stuffing mixture into ham to fill opening. Spray 9×9-inch baking pan with nonstick cooking spray; place stuffed ham in pan. Loosely spoon remaining stuffing around ham. Cover with foil. Bake for 30 minutes. Uncover and bake for additional 30 minutes, or until ham reaches an internal temperature of 155°F.

MICROWAVE DIRECTIONS:
Prepare ham and stuffing as directed above. Spray 9×9-inch microwave-safe dish with nonstick cooking spray; place stuffed ham in dish. Loosely spoon remaining stuffing around ham. Cook on High power about 9 to 10 minutes. Turn ham over; rotate pan. Continue cooking on Medium-High power (70%) about 9 to 10 minutes, or until ham reaches an internal temperature of 135°F. Cover with foil; let stand for 10 minutes, or until internal temperature reaches 155°F.

NUTRITION INFORMATION PER SERVING:
182 calories, 15.3 g protein, 4.3 g fat, 16.7 g carbohydrates, 39.2 mg cholesterol, 716 mg sodium.

BAKED HAM SLICES WITH APRICOTS

Makes 8 to 10 servings

1 Armour Lower Salt Ham Nugget (about 1¾ pounds), cut into 3-ounce slices
1 (6-ounce) package dried apricots, chopped
¾ cup no salt added chicken broth
¼ cup packed brown sugar
1 tablespoon orange flavor liqueur

Preheat oven to 350°F. Spray 13×9-inch baking dish with nonstick cooking spray; overlap ham slices in layers in dish. Combine remaining ingredients in small bowl; pour over ham slices. Bake, uncovered, for 35 minutes, or until heated through. Garnish with canned whole apricots and fresh mint leaves, if desired.

MICROWAVE DIRECTIONS:
Spray microwave-safe roasting pan with nonstick cooking spray; overlap ham slices in layers in pan. Combine remaining ingredients in small bowl; pour over ham slices. Cover with waxed paper. Cook on High power for 8 minutes; rotate pan. Cook, covered, on High power for 2 minutes, or until heated through. Garnish as above.

NUTRITION INFORMATION PER SERVING:
185 calories, 15.1 g protein, 4.1 g fat, 17.6 g carbohydrates, 39.2 mg cholesterol, 678 mg sodium.

HAM & BROCCOLI STIR-FRY

Makes 6 servings

4 tablespoons peanut oil,
  divided
2½ cups (10 ounces) Armour
  Lower Salt Ham cut into
  ¾-inch cubes
3 green onions, sliced
6 large fresh mushrooms,
  sliced
3 cups broccoli flowerets
1 (8-ounce) can sliced water
  chestnuts, drained
¼ cup Lower Salt Sweet & Sour
  Sauce (page 72)

Heat 2 tablespoons of the oil in
wok or large skillet over high heat.
Add ham; sauté until lightly
browned. Remove ham from wok;
set aside. Add remaining 2
tablespoons oil to wok and heat.
Add green onions, mushrooms
and broccoli; sauté until broccoli is
tender-crisp. Add water chestnuts
and ham cubes to vegetable
mixture, stirring to blend
ingredients. Add sweet & sour
sauce; cook until heated through.
If desired, serve over cooked rice
and garnish with red pepper
strips.

MICROWAVE DIRECTIONS:
Reduce oil to 2 tablespoons; place
in large microwave-safe dish.
Cover with vented plastic wrap;
cook on High power about 2 to 3
minutes, or until hot. Add green
onions; cook, covered, on High
power about 2 to 3 minutes, or
until tender. Add broccoli; cook,
covered, on High power about 2
to 4 minutes, or until tender-crisp.
Stir in mushrooms and water
chestnuts; cook, covered, on High
power about 1 to 2 minutes, or
until heated through. Stir in ham
and sweet & sour sauce; cook,
uncovered, on High power for 4
minutes, or until heated through.
Let stand for 3 minutes before
serving.

NUTRITION INFORMATION PER SERVING:
199 calories, 11.1 g protein, 11.8 g fat,
11.8 g carbohydrates, 23.2 mg
cholesterol, 434 mg sodium.

HAM STROGANOFF

Makes 6 servings

4 tablespoons unsalted
  margarine or butter
2 large onions, minced
1 pound fresh mushrooms,
  sliced
3 cups (12 ounces) Armour
  Lower Salt Ham cut into
  ¼-inch cubes
4 teaspoons dry mustard
½ teaspoon garlic powder
1½ cups plain nonfat yogurt
1 cup dairy sour cream

Melt margarine in large skillet
over medium-high heat. Add
vegetables; sauté until tender. Add
ham, dry mustard and garlic
powder. Reduce heat to medium;
cook until heated through.

Mix yogurt and sour cream in
small bowl. Add to ham mixture;
heat thoroughly but *do not boil*.
Serve over parslied noodles and
season with pepper, if desired.

NUTRITION INFORMATION PER SERVING:
321 calories, 19 g protein, 19.7 g fat, 16 g
carbohydrates, 46 mg cholesterol,
564 mg sodium.

Ham & Broccoli Stir-Fry

PARTY FOODS

PARTY HAM SANDWICHES

Makes 24 sandwiches

¾ cup plain nonfat yogurt
 3 teaspoons chopped fresh
    chives
 1 teaspoon dill mustard
 1 loaf party rye or
    pumpernickel bread
   Leaf lettuce, washed, torn
    and well drained
 1 Armour Lower Salt Ham
    Nugget (about 1¾ pounds),
    shaved
 1 small cucumber, thinly
    sliced
12 cherry tomatoes, cut in half

Combine yogurt, chives and
mustard in small bowl. Arrange
bread slices on serving tray;
spread evenly with yogurt
mixture. Layer lettuce, ham,
cucumber slice and tomato half on
top of each bread slice. Garnish
serving tray with lettuce and
green onions, if desired.

*NUTRITION INFORMATION PER
SANDWICH:* 101 calories, 8.4 g protein,
2.6 g fat, 10 g carbohydrates, 16.3 mg
cholesterol, 413 mg sodium.

*Top: Spicy Zucchini & Bacon
Canapes (page 52); bottom: Party
Ham Sandwiches*

SPICY ZUCCHINI & BACON CANAPES

Makes 22 to 24 canapes

1 (4-ounce) carton lowfat
  cottage cheese, well
  drained
2 green onions, finely
  chopped
½ tablespoon finely chopped
  jalapeño peppers
½ teaspoon Mrs. Dash®,
  original blend
2 medium zucchini, cut into
  ¼-inch slices
8 slices Armour Lower Salt
  Bacon, cooked crisp and
  crumbled
2 tablespoons finely chopped
  red pepper *or* 6 cherry
  tomatoes, quartered

Combine cottage cheese, green onions, jalapeño and seasoning in small bowl. Mound cottage cheese mixture evenly on top of zucchini slices; sprinkle with bacon. Top with sprinkle of red pepper or cherry tomato quarter. Garnish with fresh chives or small sprig of parsley, if desired.

NUTRITION INFORMATION PER CANAPE:
17 calories, 1.5 g protein, 0.9 g fat, 0.8 g carbohydrates, 2.4 mg cholesterol, 65.6 mg sodium.

◆◆◆

For added convenience, the cottage cheese topping for Spicy Zucchini & Bacon Canapes can be made in advance and refrigerated up to 4 hours.

ITALIAN BREAD PIZZA

Makes 12 appetizer servings

1 large loaf Italian bread
1½ cups (6 ounces) shredded
  Armour Lower Salt
  Monterey Jack Cheese,
  divided
1 (16-ounce) jar prepared no
  salt added, no sugar, no fat
  pasta sauce
1½ tablespoons dried Italian
  seasoning
12 ounces Armour Lower Salt
  Ham, thinly sliced
1 (20-ounce) can pineapple
  rings, well drained
8 thin green pepper rings
8 thin red pepper rings

Slice bread lengthwise in half. Toast cut sides under broiler until lightly browned. Sprinkle ¼ cup of the cheese on each half; broil again about 1 to 2 minutes, or until cheese is melted. Combine pasta sauce and seasoning in small saucepan; cook over medium heat until hot. Spoon sauce evenly over bread halves; top evenly with ham and pineapple rings. Place green and red pepper rings alternately on top. Sprinkle each half with ½ cup of remaining cheese; place on baking sheet. Broil 4 to 5 inches from heat source about 4 to 6 minutes, or until cheese is melted. Cut each half into 6 pieces. Garnish with parsley, if desired.

NUTRITION INFORMATION PER SERVING:
253 calories, 13.1 g protein, 6.3 g fat, 34.5 g carbohydrates, 29 mg cholesterol, 482 mg sodium.

Italian Bread Pizza

TOMATO-RICE SOUP

Makes 4 servings

1 (14½-ounce) can no salt
    added stewed tomatoes
1½ cups cooked brown rice
1 cup (4 ounces) Armour
    Lower Salt Ham cut into
    small cubes
½ cup no salt added tomato
    puree
1½ teaspoons dried chervil
1 teaspoon Mrs. Dash®,
    original blend
1 tablespoon cornstarch
2 tablespoons frozen
    unsweetened apple juice
    concentrate, thawed

Combine all ingredients *except*
cornstarch and apple juice in
medium saucepan; stir in 1 cup
water. Bring to boil over medium-
high heat; reduce heat and simmer
for 5 minutes. Blend cornstarch
and apple juice; stir into soup.
Continue cooking for 10 minutes,
or until thickened. Garnish with
croutons and fresh marjoram, if
desired.

MICROWAVE DIRECTIONS:
Combine all ingredients *except*
cornstarch and apple juice in 10-
inch microwave-safe tube pan; stir
in 1 cup water. Cover with vented
plastic wrap; cook on High power
for 10 minutes. Rotate pan and stir
soup. Mix cornstarch and apple
juice; stir into soup. Cover; cook
on High power about 7 to 10
minutes, or until thickened.
Garnish as above.

NUTRITION INFORMATION PER SERVING:
185 calories, 8.5 g protein, 1.8 g fat,
33.2 g carbohydrates, 14 mg cholesterol,
291 mg sodium.

CAJUN BACON BOWTIES

Makes 10 to 12 bowties

⅔ cup unseasoned dry bread
    crumbs
2 tablespoons Low Sodium
    Cajun Seasoning (recipe
    follows)
1 (12-ounce) package Armour
    Lower Salt Bacon
1 egg, slightly beaten

MICROWAVE DIRECTIONS:
Combine bread crumbs and
seasoning in shallow pan. Tie
loose knot in center of each bacon
slice. Combine egg and 2
tablespoons water in small bowl.
Dip bacon into egg mixture, then
into crumbs. Place 4 to 6 bacon
ties at a time in paper-towel-lined
12×10-inch microwave-safe dish;
do not overlap. Cover with paper
towel. Cook on High power for 6
minutes, or until golden brown.
Repeat with remaining bacon.

Low Sodium Cajun Seasoning:
Combine 1 tablespoon *each* black
pepper, white pepper, ground red
pepper (cayenne), onion powder
and garlic powder. Store in
airtight container.

NUTRITION INFORMATION PER BOWTIE:
66.4 calories, 3.8 g protein, 3.6 g fat,
4.9 g carbohydrates, 29.7 mg cholesterol,
193 mg sodium.

FRENCH LOAF WITH CHEESE & BACON

Makes 16 appetizer servings

16 slices Armour Lower Salt Bacon
2 medium green peppers, chopped
1 large onion, chopped
5 medium-size fresh mushrooms, sliced
1 large loaf French bread
1 cup prepared no salt added, no sugar, no fat pasta sauce
1 tablespoon dried Italian seasoning
1 clove garlic, finely chopped
1 cup (4 ounces) shredded Armour Lower Salt Monterey Jack Cheese

Tie loose knot in center of each bacon slice. Cook until crisp; set aside. Spray large skillet with nonstick cooking spray. Add vegetables; sauté until tender. Drain well. Slice bread lengthwise in half. Mix pasta sauce, seasoning and garlic. Spread ½ cup of the sauce mixture over each bread half. Divide vegetables evenly over sauce. Sprinkle ½ cup of the cheese over each half. Broil 4 to 5 inches from heat source about 2 to 3 minutes, or until cheese is bubbly and lightly browned. Lay 8 bacon ties, evenly spaced, on each half. Turn oven off; return loaves to oven 5 minutes to warm bacon. Cut each half into 8 pieces.

NUTRITION INFORMATION PER SERVING: 154 calories, 7.1 g protein, 5.6 g fat, 18.7 g carbohydrates, 13.5 mg cholesterol, 315 mg sodium.

HAM MANICOTTI

Makes 5 to 7 servings

1 (8-ounce) package uncooked manicotti shells
½ Armour Lower Salt Ham Nugget (about 14 ounces), cut into julienne strips
1½ cups chopped fresh spinach, washed and well drained
1 (16-ounce) jar prepared no salt added, no sugar, no fat pasta sauce
2 teaspoons dried Italian seasoning
4 green onions, sliced
1 cup (4 ounces) shredded Armour Lower Salt Monterey Jack Cheese

Preheat oven to 400°F. Spray 13×9-inch pan with nonstick cooking spray. Stuff uncooked manicotti shells with ham strips; place in single layer in pan. Sprinkle spinach over top of shells. Mix pasta sauce, 1¼ cups water and seasoning in medium bowl; pour over spinach. Sprinkle green onions over sauce. Cover with waxed paper and seal with foil. Bake for 45 minutes, or until pasta is tender. Uncover; sprinkle with cheese. Broil 4 to 5 inches from heat source about 2 to 4 minutes, or until cheese is melted.

NUTRITION INFORMATION PER SERVING: 303 calories, 20.2 g protein, 8.6 g fat, 33 g carbohydrates, 45 mg cholesterol, 572 mg sodium.

———◆◆◆———

Prepare a double batch of Ham Manicotti and freeze half for a future party.

Ham Manicotti

SPICY HOT DOG CORN BISCUITS

Makes 16 to 20 appetizer servings

4 to 5 Armour Lower Salt Jumbo Beef Hot Dogs
1 (7½-ounce) package corn bread mix, plus ingredients to prepare mix
2 tablespoons finely chopped red pepper
2 teaspoons chili powder

Preheat oven to 400°F. Cut each hot dog crosswise into fourths. Prepare corn bread mix according to package directions; fold red pepper and chili powder into batter. Spray large baking sheet with nonstick cooking spray. Drop about three fourths of the batter into 16 to 20 mounds onto pan. Press 1 hot dog chunk into center of each mound. Top hot dog chunks with small amount of remaining batter. Bake about 8 to 10 minutes, or until golden brown. Serve with fresh salsa or honey, if desired.

NUTRITION INFORMATION PER SERVING:
87.5 calories, 2.9 g protein, 4.7 g fat, 8.5 g carbohydrates, 19.7 mg cholesterol, 213 mg sodium.

Spicy Hot Dog Corn Biscuits and hot vegetable soup make a satisfying meal.

HAM CUBES WITH DIPPING SAUCES

Makes 16 to 20 appetizer servings

Assorted Dipping Sauces (recipes follow)
2 Armour Lower Salt Ham Nuggets (about 1¾ pounds each), cut into 1-inch cubes
Leaf lettuce, washed and well drained

Prepare dipping sauces as desired. Arrange ham cubes on lettuce-lined platter; place small bowls of sauces around platter. Serve with party toothpicks.

NUTRITION INFORMATION PER 1 OUNCE SERVING OF HAM (sauces not included):
41 calories, 5.1 g protein, 1.4 g fat, 0.4 g carbohydrates, 14 mg cholesterol, 240 mg sodium.

HOT CHEESE SAUCE

Prepare jalapeño variation of Lower Salt Cheese Sauce (page 13). Serve immediately. Garnish with green onion curls, if desired.

NUTRITION INFORMATION PER TEASPOON: 10.3 calories, 0.5 g protein, 0.8 g fat, 0.3 g carbohydrates, 1.7 mg cholesterol, 7.9 mg sodium.

Spicy Hot Dog Corn Biscuits

RASPBERRY-BANANA SAUCE

1 (18-ounce) jar raspberry jam
1 medium banana
2 tablespoons raspberry schnapps

Place jam and banana in food processor or blender; process until smooth. Pour into small saucepan; cook over medium heat until bubbly and hot. Stir in schnapps; cool slightly. Pour into serving bowl. Garnish with fresh mint leaves, if desired.

NUTRITION INFORMATION PER TEASPOON: 11.8 calories, 0 g protein, 0 g fat, 2.6 g carbohydrates, 0 mg cholesterol, 0.01 mg sodium.

KIWI SAUCE

6 kiwifruit, peeled
1/2 cup sugar
1/4 teaspoon lime juice
1/4 cup evaporated skim milk, partially frozen

Place kiwifruit in food processor or blender; process until smooth. Add sugar and lime juice; process until sugar is dissolved. Add slushy milk; process until slightly thickened. Pour into chilled serving bowl. Garnish with fresh lime slices and mint leaves, if desired.

NUTRITION INFORMATION PER TEASPOON: 5.9 calories, 0.1 g protein, 0.1 g fat, 1.5 g carbohydrates, 0.02 mg cholesterol, 0.8 mg sodium.

HAM BUNDLES ON STRAWBERRY DELIGHT

Makes 4 servings

1 cup unsweetened frozen strawberries, partially thawed
1/2 cup (4 ounces) light cream cheese, softened
1/4 cup sugar
2 tablespoons skim milk
8 (1-ounce) slices Armour Lower Salt Ham
10 (12-inch) whole fresh chives
3/4 cup slivered blanched almonds

Place strawberries in blender or food processor; process until smooth. Add cream cheese, sugar and milk; process until sugar is dissolved. Refrigerate until ready to use.

Loosely roll up ham slices; tie each with 1 chive strand. Cut remaining 2 chives and use to decorate bundles. Divide strawberry mixture evenly among 4 dessert plates. Place 2 ham bundles in center of sauce; sprinkle with almonds. Serve immediately.

NUTRITION INFORMATION PER SERVING: 353 calories, 18.1 g protein, 21.2 g fat, 21.7 g carbohydrates, 53 mg cholesterol, 601 mg sodium.

◆◆◆

To quickly soften cream cheese, remove from foil packaging. Place on microwave-safe plate and cover with vented plastic wrap. Cook on High power about 25 to 35 seconds.

Ham Bundles on Strawberry Delight

SAUCY COCKTAIL FRANKS

Makes 10 appetizer servings

1 (16-ounce) package Armour
  Lower Salt Jumbo Beef
  Hot Dogs
1 (15¼-ounce) can pineapple
  chunks, drained
½ cup Lower Salt Sweet & Sour
  Sauce (page 72)
2 tablespoons chopped green
  pepper

Cut each hot dog crosswise into
fourths. Combine all ingredients
in large saucepan over medium
heat; cook until bubbly and hot.
Garnish with parsley or green
pepper rings, if desired.

MICROWAVE DIRECTIONS:

Cut each hot dog crosswise into
fourths. Combine all ingredients
in large microwave-safe casserole.
Cook, covered, on High power
about 4 to 6 minutes, or until hot
dogs are heated through, stirring
once during cooking. Garnish as
above.

NUTRITION INFORMATION PER SERVING:
186 calories, 5.7 g protein, 12 g fat,
14.8 g carbohydrates, 24 mg cholesterol,
368 mg sodium.

◆◆◆

*Saucy Cocktail Franks make a
delightful filling for a pita
sandwich.*

HAM & PEAR CUSTARD FINALE

Makes 4 servings

1 (0.8-ounce) package
  sugar free vanilla pudding
  & pie filling mix
2 cups skim milk
2 tablespoons orange flavor
  liqueur
1 (8¼-ounce) can no sugar
  added lite pear halves,
  undrained
4 ounces Armour Lower Salt
  Ham, thinly sliced and cut
  into strips
4 (¾-inch) slices frozen pound
  cake, thawed

Prepare pudding according to
package directions using skim
milk. Allow to almost set-up at
room temperature. Stir in liqueur.
Heat pear halves with juice in
small saucepan over medium heat;
drain well. Keep warm. Heat ham
in top of double boiler about 5 to
7 minutes, or until hot.

Pour ¼ cup of the custard sauce
onto each of 4 dessert plates. Place
1 cake slice on top of sauce.
Arrange ¼ cup of the warm ham
over cake; place pear half on ham.
Drizzle 2 tablespoons custard
sauce over pear. Garnish with
lemon zest and mint sprig, if
desired.

NUTRITION INFORMATION PER SERVING:
291 calories, 11.6 g protein, 8.9 g fat,
38.2 g carbohydrates, 178 mg
cholesterol, 535 mg sodium.

Ham & Pear Custard Finale

ETHNIC FLAVORS

BACON NACHOS

Makes 4 to 6 servings

8 ounces salt-free tortilla
   chips
1 (12-ounce) package Armour
   Lower Salt Bacon, slices
   cooked crisp and crumbled
½ cup sliced green onions
1 medium tomato, seeded and
   chopped
3 tablespoons sliced jalapeño
   peppers
2 tablespoons sliced ripe
   olives
¾ cup (3 ounces) shredded
   Armour Lower Salt
   Cheddar Cheese

Preheat oven to 350°F. Spread half
the tortilla chips on heatproof
plate. Layer with half the bacon,
green onions, tomato, peppers,
olives and cheese. Add second
layer of chips; top with remaining
ingredients. Bake about 5 to 7
minutes, or until cheese is melted.
Serve with salsa or guacamole, if
desired.

MICROWAVE DIRECTIONS:
Assemble nachos as directed
above, using a microwave-safe
plate. Cook on High power for 2
minutes, or until cheese is melted.

NUTRITION INFORMATION PER SERVING:
181 calories, 12.6 g protein, 18.7 g fat,
27.1 g carbohydrates, 33 mg cholesterol,
560 mg sodium.

POLYNESIAN KABOBS

Makes 8 kabobs

3 cups (12 ounces) Armour
   Lower Salt Ham cut into
   1-inch cubes
1 fresh pineapple, peeled and
   cut into 1-inch cubes
1 green, red and yellow
   pepper, each cut into
   1-inch pieces
8 medium-size fresh
   mushrooms
¼ cup bottled low calorie, low
   sodium red wine vinegar
   salad dressing *or* Lower
   Salt Sweet & Sour Sauce
   (page 72)

Preheat oven to 350°F. Thread
ham, pineapple, peppers and
mushrooms onto 8 (10-inch) metal
or wooden skewers, alternating
the ingredients. Place in baking
dish. Brush all sides with dressing.
Bake for 8 minutes. Turn kabobs
and baste all sides with dressing.
Cook about 6 to 8 minutes, or
until ham is heated through. Serve
over rice, if desired.

MICROWAVE DIRECTIONS:
Assemble kabobs as directed
above, using 10-inch wooden
skewers. Place in large, shallow
microwave-safe casserole dish;
brush all sides with dressing.
Cover with vented plastic wrap.
Cook on Medium-High power
(70%) about 7 to 9 minutes, or
until ham is heated through. Serve
over rice, if desired.

NUTRITION INFORMATION PER KABOB:
132.5 calories, 8.9 g protein, 2.3 g fat,
18.3 g carbohydrates, 21 mg cholesterol,
368 mg sodium.

GERMAN PANCAKE WITH BACON

Makes 4 servings

1 cup all-purpose flour
¾ teaspoon low sodium baking
   powder
1 cup skim milk
6 eggs, slightly beaten
2 teaspoons vegetable oil
8 slices Armour Lower Salt
   Bacon, cooked crisp
3 cups frozen or fresh mixed
   fruit, thawed if frozen

Preheat oven to 425°F. Combine
flour and baking powder in large
bowl. Stir in milk and eggs. Brush
oil on bottom and side of 10-inch
ovenproof skillet. Pour batter all at
once into skillet. Arrange bacon
spoke-fashion on batter. Bake,
uncovered, about 20 to 25
minutes, or until pancake is puffed
and golden brown. Top with fruit;
cut into wedges. Serve
immediately.

NUTRITION INFORMATION PER SERVING:
388 calories, 19.3 g protein, 16.8 g fat,
41.2 g carbohydrates, 424 mg
cholesterol, 390 mg sodium.

*For a lower cholesterol dish, use
1¼ cups egg substitute in place of
the 6 eggs in German Pancake with
Bacon.*

German Pancake with Bacon

BACON & BROCCOLI FRITTATA

Makes 4 servings

6 eggs, beaten
¼ cup skim milk
⅛ teaspoon white pepper
2 tablespoons unsalted
    margarine or butter
1 cup fresh or frozen broccoli
    flowerets, thawed if
    frozen
¼ cup *each* chopped red and
    green pepper
8 slices Armour Lower Salt
    Bacon, cooked crisp
1 cup (4 ounces) shredded
    Armour Lower Salt
    Cheddar Cheese

Preheat oven to 350°F. Combine
eggs, milk and white pepper in
medium bowl; set aside. Melt
margarine in large ovenproof
skillet or metal casserole over
medium heat. Add broccoli and
red and green peppers; sauté for 5
minutes. Pour egg mixture over
vegetables. Arrange bacon on top;
sprinkle with cheese. Bake about
15 to 20 minutes, or until cheese is
melted and eggs are set. Cut and
serve immediately. Garnish with
halved cherry tomatoes and
parsley, if desired.

NUTRITION INFORMATION PER SERVING:
360 calories, 22 g protein, 29 g fat, 6.1 g
carbohydrates, 453 mg cholesterol,
478 mg sodium.

INDIAN RICE SALAD

Makes 4 to 6 servings

½ cup plain nonfat yogurt
¼ cup chutney
3 cups cooked rice
2 cups (8 ounces) Armour
    Lower Salt Ham cut into
    ½-inch cubes
2 medium-size red apples,
    cored, unpeeled and
    chopped
½ cup sliced celery
½ cup raisins
2 tablespoons slivered
    almonds, toasted

Combine yogurt and chutney in
small bowl. Combine remaining
ingredients in large bowl. Pour
chutney mixture over rice mixture;
mix well. Cover; refrigerate at
least 1 hour before serving to
blend flavors. Serve on leaf lettuce
and garnish with celery leaves, if
desired.

NUTRITION INFORMATION PER SERVING:
278 calories, 10.8 g protein, 3.4 g fat,
49.5 g carbohydrates, 19 mg cholesterol,
370 mg sodium.

---

*To toast almonds in microwave
oven, melt 1 teaspoon unsalted
margarine or butter in microwave-
safe tray or dish. Spread 2
tablespoons almonds in single layer
in margarine; toss gently to coat.
Cook on High power about 2 to 3
minutes.*

BAKED PAPAYA WITH HAM FILLING

Makes 4 servings

1½ tablespoons unsalted
    margarine or butter
½ cup sliced green onions
2 cloves garlic, crushed
1 cup (4 ounces) Armour
    Lower Salt Ham cut into
    julienne strips
1 medium tomato, seeded and
    chopped
2 ripe papayas (about 1 pound
    each), cut lengthwise in
    half and seeded
    Boiling water
½ cup (2 ounces) shredded
    Armour Lower Salt
    Monterey Jack Cheese

Preheat oven to 350°F. Melt margarine in medium skillet over medium heat. Add green onions and garlic; sauté about 3 to 5 minutes, or until tender. Stir in ham and tomato. Cook about 4 to 6 minutes, or until tomato is soft. Spoon ham mixture evenly into papaya shells. Arrange shells in shallow roasting pan; add enough boiling water to come 1 inch up sides of papayas. Bake, uncovered, about 25 to 35 minutes, or until papaya pierces easily with fork. Drain liquid from pan; sprinkle papayas with cheese. Broil 2 to 3 inches from heat source about 2 to 3 minutes, or until cheese is melted. Garnish with fresh mint leaves, if desired.

MICROWAVE DIRECTIONS:
Omit boiling water. Place margarine in medium microwave-safe dish. Cook on High power for 30 seconds. Add green onions and garlic; cook, covered, on High power for 3 minutes, or until onion is tender. Stir in ham and tomato. Spoon ham mixture evenly into papaya shells. Arrange shells in 8×8-inch microwave-safe dish; cover with waxed paper. Cook on Medium-High power (70%) about 10 to 12 minutes, or until papaya pierces easily with fork. Sprinkle with cheese; cook on High power about 1 to 2 minutes, or until cheese is melted. Garnish as above.

NUTRITION INFORMATION PER SERVING:
203 calories, 10.1 g protein, 10.6 g fat, 18.2 g carbohydrates, 29 mg cholesterol, 303 mg sodium.

BACON TACOS

Makes 8 tacos

8 taco shells
    Leaf lettuce *or* shredded
    iceberg lettuce
12 slices Armour Lower Salt
    Bacon, cut in half and
    cooked crisp
1 medium tomato, seeded and
    chopped
3 green onions, thinly sliced
½ cup (2 ounces) shredded
    Armour Lower Salt
    Cheddar Cheese

Preheat oven to 350°F. Place taco shells on baking sheet; bake for 5 minutes. Divide leaf lettuce, bacon, tomato, green onions and cheese evenly among shells. Serve with salsa, if desired.

NUTRITION INFORMATION PER TACO:
128 calories, 6.2 g protein, 8.1 g fat, 8.6 g carbohydrates, 16.5 mg cholesterol, 289.5 mg sodium.

Baked Papaya with Ham Filling

CUBAN BLACK BEAN & HAM SOUP

Makes 4 servings

1 cup uncooked black beans, soaked overnight and drained
1 (2-ounce) slice Armour Lower Salt Ham
1/2 cup chopped green pepper
1 medium onion, finely chopped
2 teaspoons Mrs. Dash®, original blend
1 teaspoon garlic powder
1 teaspoon ground cumin
1/4 teaspoon black pepper
1 1/2 cups (6 ounces) Armour Lower Salt Ham cut into 3/4-inch cubes

Combine beans, ham slice, green pepper, onion and seasonings in medium saucepan; add enough water to just cover beans. Bring to boil; reduce heat, cover and simmer about 1 1/2 to 2 hours, or until beans are tender and most of liquid is absorbed. Add ham cubes. Cook 10 minutes, or until ham is heated through. Remove ham slice before serving. Serve over rice, if desired.

NUTRITION INFORMATION PER SERVING: 244 calories, 20.2 g protein, 3.5 g fat, 30.5 g carbohydrates, 28 mg cholesterol, 489 mg sodium.

———◆◆◆———

If you forget to soak beans overnight, here's a time-saving solution: Add 1 cup beans to 6 cups water. Bring to a boil; reduce heat and simmer 2 minutes. Remove from heat. Cover and let stand at least 1 hour; drain.

LOWER SALT SWEET & SOUR SAUCE

Makes 3 cups

1 cup rice or white vinegar
3/4 cup packed brown sugar
1/2 cup no salt added tomato puree
1/2 cup pineapple juice
1 tablespoon lite soy sauce
1 clove garlic, crushed
1/4 cup cornstarch

Combine vinegar and brown sugar in small saucepan. Bring to boil over medium heat. Reduce heat; simmer until sugar is dissolved, stirring frequently. Stir in tomato puree, pineapple juice, 1/2 cup water, soy sauce and garlic. Simmer 10 minutes. Combine cornstarch and 1/4 cup water; stir into sauce mixture. Cook over low heat, stirring constantly, about 2 to 3 minutes, or until thickened.

NUTRITION INFORMATION PER 1/4 CUP: 110.5 calories, 0.5 g protein, 0 g fat, 30.5 g carbohydrates, 0 mg cholesterol, 84.5 mg sodium.

———◆◆◆———

Prepare Lower Salt Sweet & Sour Sauce and keep on hand for extra convenience. Store it in an airtight container in the refrigerator for up to three weeks.

Cuban Black Bean & Ham Soup

HAM CURRIED RICE

Makes 4 servings

1 tablespoon unsalted
    margarine or butter
½ cup thinly sliced celery
¼ cup sliced green onions
2 teaspoons curry powder
1 cup uncooked rice*
2 teaspoons no salt added
    chicken flavor instant
    bouillon
2½ cups (10 ounces) Armour
    Lower Salt Ham cut into
    ½-inch cubes
1 (14½-ounce) can no salt
    added stewed tomatoes,
    undrained

Melt margarine in medium saucepan over medium heat. Add celery, green onions and curry powder. Sauté about 3 to 5 minutes, or until celery is tender. Stir in rice, bouillon, 1¼ cups water, ham and tomatoes. Bring to boil; reduce heat to simmer. Cook, covered, about 25 to 35 minutes, or until liquid is absorbed. Garnish with unsalted cashew halves, if desired.

MICROWAVE DIRECTIONS:

Place margarine in large microwave-safe casserole dish. Cook on High power for 30 seconds. Add celery, green onions, curry powder, *instant* rice, bouillon, 1 cup water, ham and tomatoes. Cover with vented plastic wrap. Cook on High power about 8 to 10 minutes, or until liquid is absorbed, stirring twice during cooking. Garnish as above.

NUTRITION INFORMATION PER SERVING:
345 calories, 17.2 g protein, 7.4 g fat, 48.5 g carbohydrates, 35.5 mg cholesterol, 665 mg sodium.

ORIENTAL CUCUMBER SALAD

Makes 4 servings

2 cups (8 ounces) Armour
    Lower Salt Ham cut into
    ½-inch cubes
2 medium cucumbers,
    unpeeled and thinly sliced
8 cherry tomatoes, cut into
    fourths
2 green onions, thinly sliced
¼ cup bottled low calorie, low
    sodium red wine vinegar
    salad dressing
1 tablespoon sesame seed oil
¼ teaspoon hot pepper sauce

Combine all ingredients in medium bowl; toss to coat well. Cover; refrigerate at least 1 hour before serving. Toss every 15 minutes for the first hour of chilling to blend flavors. Garnish with green onion flower, if desired.

NUTRITION INFORMATION PER SERVING:
128 calories, 10.3 g protein, 6.3 g fat, 3.9 g carbohydrates, 28 mg cholesterol, 495 mg sodium.

*Use 1 cup uncooked *instant* rice in microwave directions.

Ham Curried Rice

HOT HAWAIIAN POTATO SALAD

Makes 6 servings

4 tablespoons unsalted margarine or butter, divided
1 cup thinly sliced celery
1 green pepper, chopped
⅓ cup chopped red onion
2 tablespoons all-purpose flour
1 (15¼-ounce) can pineapple chunks, drained and juice reserved
¼ cup cider vinegar
2 cups (8 ounces) Armour Lower Salt Ham cut into ½-inch cubes
6 medium potatoes, cooked and diced

Preheat oven to 350°F. Melt 2 tablespoons margarine in large skillet over medium heat. Add celery, green pepper and onion; sauté until tender. Remove from skillet; set aside.

Melt remaining 2 tablespoons margarine in skillet over medium heat. Stir in flour to make a paste. Add enough water to reserved pineapple juice to make 1 cup. Gradually stir into paste; add vinegar. Bring to boil, stirring constantly, until thickened. Combine ham, potatoes, pineapple chunks and onion mixture in large casserole dish. Gently stir in hot dressing. Bake about 15 to 20 minutes, or until ham is heated through. Garnish with parsley, if desired.

MICROWAVE DIRECTIONS:
Place 4 tablespoons margarine in large microwave-safe dish. Cook on High power for 1 minute. Stir in flour to make a paste. Add enough water to reserved pineapple juice to make 1 cup. Gradually stir into paste; add vinegar. Cover with vented plastic wrap; cook on High power about 3 to 5 minutes, or until thickened. Add celery, green pepper, onion, ham, potatoes and pineapple chunks. Cook, covered, on Medium-High power (70%) about 4 to 6 minutes, or until ham is heated through. Garnish as above.

NUTRITION INFORMATION PER SERVING: 302 calories, 9.7 g protein, 10.1 g fat, 44 g carbohydrates, 18.6 mg cholesterol, 345 mg sodium.

◆◆◆

Sprinkle eight slices of crisp, crumbled Armour Lower Salt Bacon over Hot Hawaiian Potato Salad for added flavor and color.

Hot Hawaiian Potato Salad

IRISH SODA BACON BREAD

Makes 12 to 15 servings

4 cups all-purpose flour
3 tablespoons sugar
1½ tablespoons low sodium
    baking powder
1 teaspoon baking soda
6 tablespoons unsalted
    margarine or butter, cold
1 cup golden raisins
6 slices Armour Lower Salt
    Bacon, cooked crisp and
    crumbled
2 eggs
1½ cups buttermilk

Preheat oven to 375°F. Combine flour, sugar, baking powder and soda in large bowl; cut in margarine until mixture resembles coarse crumbs. Stir in raisins and bacon. Beat eggs slightly in small bowl; remove and reserve 1 tablespoon egg. Add buttermilk and remaining eggs to flour mixture; stir to make soft dough. Turn out onto lightly floured surface; knead about 1 to 2 minutes, or until smooth.

Shape dough into round loaf. Spray round 2-quart casserole dish with nonstick cooking spray; place dough in dish. With floured knife, cut a 4-inch cross about ¼-inch deep on top of loaf. Brush loaf with reserved egg. Bake about 55 to 65 minutes, or until toothpick inserted into center comes out clean. (Cover loaf with foil during last 30 minutes of baking to prevent overbrowning.) Cool on wire rack 10 minutes; remove from dish. Serve with light cream cheese or honey butter, if desired.

NUTRITION INFORMATION PER SERVING: 231 calories, 6.2 g protein, 7 g fat, 36.7 g carbohydrates, 39.7 mg cholesterol, 130 mg sodium.

━━━━━━━━━━━━◆◆◆━━━━━━━━━━━━

To easily crumble cooked bacon, place slices in food processor with metal blade. Process until finely crumbled.

NAVY BEAN SOUP

Makes 4 servings

2 tablespoons vegetable oil
1 cup chopped leeks
1½ cups (6 ounces) Armour
    Lower Salt Ham cut into
    ½-inch cubes
1 cup uncooked navy beans,
    soaked overnight and
    drained
1 tablespoon chopped
    jalapeño peppers

Heat oil in 3-quart saucepan over medium heat. Add leeks; sauté about 3 to 5 minutes, or until tender. Stir in ham, beans and peppers; add enough water to just cover beans. Bring to boil; reduce heat, cover and simmer about 1 to 1½ hours, or until beans are tender.

NUTRITION INFORMATION PER SERVING: 282 calories, 17.5 g protein, 9.9 g fat, 30.2 g carbohydrates, 21 mg cholesterol, 420 mg sodium.

Irish Soda Bacon Bread

FOR KIDS OF ALL AGES

HAM & CHEESE PASTRY CUTOUTS

Makes 25 to 27 pastries

1 **Armour Lower Salt Ham Nugget (about 1³/₄ pounds)**
1 **(17¹/₄-ounce) package frozen puff pastry (2 sheets)**
1³/₄ **cups (7 ounces) shredded Armour Lower Salt Cheddar Cheese**
¹/₂ **cup finely chopped green onions**

Preheat oven to 350°F. Cut ham into about 27 (1-ounce) slices. Use animal or other favorite cookie cutters to cut ham slices into shapes. Roll each pastry sheet to 14-inch square on floured surface. Cut into circles, squares or rectangles to fit shapes of ham cutouts. Spray baking sheet with nonstick cooking spray; place pastry on sheet. Prick with fork to keep pastry from bubbling up. Bake for 10 minutes. Sprinkle with small amount of cheese and green onions; top with ham cutouts. Continue baking about 5 to 7 minutes, or until cheese is melted and ham is warm.

NUTRITION INFORMATION PER PASTRY: 148 calories, 8 g protein, 8.8 g fat, 7.3 g carbohydrates, 22.2 mg cholesterol, 362 mg sodium.

HOT DOG BISCUIT BITES

Makes 40 wedges

¼ cup plain nonfat yogurt
2 tablespoons chopped onion
½ tablespoon prepared
    mustard
1 (7½-ounce) package
    refrigerated buttermilk
    biscuits
2 to 3 Armour Lower Salt
    Jumbo Meat Hot Dogs,
    thinly sliced
3 tablespoons low sodium
    catsup

Preheat oven to 375°F. Combine yogurt, onion and mustard in small bowl; mix well. Cut each biscuit into 4 wedges. Flatten each wedge out with bottom of a glass. Spread yogurt mixture on wedges; press 1 hot dog slice in center of each. Spray baking sheet with nonstick cooking spray; place wedges on sheet. Bake about 8 to 10 minutes, or until puffy and golden brown. Top with small amount of catsup.

NUTRITION INFORMATION PER WEDGE:
23 calories, 0.8 g protein, 0.9 g fat, 2.9 g carbohydrates, 1.5 mg cholesterol, 75.4 mg sodium.

Make Hot Dog Biscuit Bites ahead and freeze. Let the kids reheat them for a healthy after-school snack.

CORN BREAD AND BACON BATTER BAKE

Makes 6 servings

1 (7½-ounce) package corn
    bread mix, plus
    ingredients to prepare mix
2 Armour Lower Salt Jumbo
    Meat Hot Dogs, cut
    crosswise into thirds
3 slices Armour Lower Salt
    Bacon, cooked crisp and
    crumbled
½ cup (2 ounces) shredded
    Armour Lower Salt
    Cheddar Cheese

Preheat oven to 400°F. Prepare corn bread mix according to package directions. Spray 10-inch ovenproof skillet or 8×8-inch baking pan with nonstick cooking spray; pour in batter. Stand hot dog chunk on 1 end. Cut down into hot dog almost to the end. (Do not cut all the way through.) Make another cut into hot dog, like the first, to form crisscross. Repeat with all hot dog chunks. Place hot dogs cut side up into batter 2 inches from side of pan, arranging in circle. Bake about 18 to 25 minutes, or until toothpick inserted into corn bread comes out clean. Sprinkle bacon and cheese over top. Let stand for 5 minutes before serving.

NUTRITION INFORMATION PER SERVING:
283 calories, 10.3 g protein, 14.6 g fat, 27.5 g carbohydrates, 69 mg cholesterol, 656 mg sodium.

Corn Bread and Bacon Batter Bake

HOT & SPICY DOGS

Makes 2 servings

2 Armour Lower Salt Jumbo
  Meat Hot Dogs
½ cup Lower Salt Sweet & Sour
  Sauce (page 72)
1 dash hot pepper sauce
1 bagel, cut in half and toasted
2 tablespoons light cream
  cheese, softened

Cut hot dogs crosswise, three fourths of the way through, every ½ inch. Heat in small saucepan of boiling water for 2 minutes. (Hot dogs will curl as they heat.) Drain; set aside. Heat sweet & sour sauce with hot pepper sauce in small saucepan. Add hot dogs; heat about 1 to 2 minutes. Spread each bagel half with 1 tablespoon cream cheese; place curled hot dog over cheese. Serve with pineapple spears, if desired.

MICROWAVE DIRECTIONS:
Cut hot dogs as directed above; place on paper towels. Cook on High power for 1 minute. Combine sweet & sour sauce and hot pepper sauce in small microwave-safe dish; cover with vented plastic wrap. Cook on High power for 1 minute. Add hot dogs; cook, covered, on High power for 30 seconds or until hot. Assemble as above.

NUTRITION INFORMATION PER SERVING:
403 calories, 12 g protein, 19 g fat, 48 g carbohydrates, 42.5 mg cholesterol, 696 mg sodium.

Hot & Spicy Dogs also taste great on cinnamon-raisin bagels.

OPEN-FACED BACON SANDWICHES

Makes 2 servings

2 hamburger buns, toasted
½ cup (2 ounces) shredded
  Armour Lower Salt
  Cheddar Cheese
2 thinly sliced red pepper
  rings
2 thinly sliced green pepper
  rings
4 slices Armour Lower Salt
  Bacon, cooked crisp and
  finely crumbled

Sprinkle each bun half with one fourth of the cheese. Place 1 pepper ring on each bun. Divide bacon into 4 equal portions; sprinkle on buns. Broil 4 to 6 inches from heat source or in toaster oven about 1 to 2 minutes, or until cheese is melted.

MICROWAVE DIRECTIONS:
Assemble sandwiches as directed above. Place on large microwave-safe plate. Cook on Medium-High power (70%) about 30 to 45 seconds, or until cheese is melted.

NUTRITION INFORMATION PER SERVING:
294 calories, 14.3 g protein, 15.8 g fat, 22.8 g carbohydrates, 42 mg cholesterol, 599 mg sodium.

Plan Ham Animal Salads for a child's birthday party. Kids love to eat their own food creations.

HAM ANIMAL SALADS

Makes 6 servings

- 2 Armour Lower Salt Jumbo Meat Hot Dogs
  Leaf lettuce, washed and drained
- 6 (1-ounce) slices Armour Lower Salt Ham
- 1/2 cup flaked coconut
- 1/2 cup *each* golden and dark raisins
- 1 (8-ounce) package dried mixed fruit
- 1 cup miniature marshmallows
- 5 to 10 large marshmallows
- 2 teaspoons *each* red, green and yellow sugar-free gelatin

Cut hot dogs crosswise, three fourths of the way through, every 1/2 inch. Heat in small saucepan of boiling water for 2 minutes. (Hot dogs will curl as they heat.) Drain; set aside.

Create animal salads as follows: Place lettuce on individual serving plates. Cut animal shapes out of ham slices with cookie cutters. Use remaining ingredients to decorate animals. Try bits of raisins and dried fruit for eyes or spots. Use coconut for hair. Cut marshmallows and dip in dry gelatin for ears. Create fences around animals using hot dog

curls, or make dragons using toothpicks and raisins for spiny backs. Use any of the decorative foods to garnish your animal picture. (You may not use all of the decorative foods.)

NUTRITION INFORMATION PER SERVING: 345 calories, 10.6 g protein, 9 g fat, 58 g carbohydrates, 24 mg cholesterol, 473 mg sodium.

CRISP BACON AND JELLY SANDWICHES

Makes 2 servings

- 4 slices whole wheat bread
- 2 ounces light cream cheese, softened
- 2 tablespoons apple-cinnamon jelly
- 4 slices Armour Lower Salt Bacon, cooked crisp
- 2 tablespoons unsalted margarine or butter, melted

Spread 1 side of each bread slice with cream cheese. Spread 1 tablespoon jelly on each of 2 slices; top each with 2 bacon strips. Top with remaining bread slices, cheese side down. Brush both sides of sandwiches with margarine. Cook in large skillet over medium-high heat about 2 to 3 minutes on each side, or until crisp and brown.

NUTRITION INFORMATION PER SERVING: 411 calories, 13.1 g protein, 25.7 g fat, 38.4 g carbohydrates, 37 mg cholesterol, 685 mg sodium.

CORN MUFFINS WITH HOT DOG STARS

Makes 12 muffins

1 (7½-ounce) package corn
   bread mix, plus
   ingredients to prepare mix
1 tablespoon finely chopped
   onion
½ tablespoon finely chopped
   jalapeño peppers
3 Armour Lower Salt Jumbo
   Meat Hot Dogs, cut
   crosswise into fourths
¼ cup (1 ounce) shredded
   Armour Lower Salt
   Cheddar Cheese

Preheat oven to 400°F. Prepare
corn bread mix according to
package directions, stirring in
onion and peppers with liquid.
Line 12 muffin tin cups with
paper baking cups; spoon batter
evenly into cups.

To cut hot dog stars, stand hot dog
chunk on 1 end. Cut down into
hot dog almost to the end. (Do not
cut all the way through.) Make
another cut into hot dog, like the
first, to form crisscross. Repeat
with all hot dog chunks. Place
uncut end of 1 hot dog down into
middle of each muffin cup. Bake
about 15 to 17 minutes, or until
toothpick inserted into muffin
comes out clean. (Hot dog will
form curled star while baking.)
Top with cheese.

NUTRITION INFORMATION PER MUFFIN:
139 calories, 4.7 g protein, 7.3 g fat,
13.8 g carbohydrates, 33 mg cholesterol,
333 mg sodium.

CHEESY HOT DOG PACKAGES

Makes 12 packages

3 Armour Lower Salt Jumbo
   Beef Hot Dogs
1 (8-ounce) package
   refrigerated crescent rolls
½ cup (2 ounces) shredded
   Armour Lower Salt
   Cheddar Cheese

Preheat oven to 375°F. Cut each
hot dog crosswise into fourths.
Unroll crescent dough into 4
pieces. Roll each piece into a solid
8×5-inch sheet, using rolling pin.
Cut each sheet crosswise into
thirds. Place hot dog piece in
center of each dough portion;
sprinkle with cheese. Gather
dough up over hot dog to form
small package; pinch dough
together to seal. Spray baking
sheet with nonstick cooking spray;
place packages on sheet. Bake for
10 minutes, or until golden
brown. Serve with fresh salsa, if
desired.

NUTRITION INFORMATION PER PACKAGE:
127 calories, 3.9 g protein, 8.9 g fat, 8 g
carbohydrates, 12.5 mg cholesterol,
281 mg sodium.

*Cheesy Hot Dog Packages are a
fast snack for unexpected company.*

CHEESY VEGETABLE SCRAMBLED EGGS

Makes 2 servings

1 tablespoon unsalted
   margarine or butter
1 green onion, sliced
1 tablespoon *each* chopped red
   and green pepper
2 eggs, slightly beaten
1 Armour Lower Salt Jumbo
   Meat Hot Dog, sliced
¼ cup (1 ounce) shredded
   Armour Lower Salt
   Cheddar Cheese

Melt margarine in small skillet over medium-high heat. Add vegetables; sauté for 1 minute. Add eggs; reduce heat to medium-low and cook for 2 minutes. Stir in hot dog slices. Continue cooking until eggs are almost set; sprinkle with cheese. Cook for 1 minute, or until cheese is melted. Garnish with green and red pepper strips and parsley, if desired.

MICROWAVE DIRECTIONS:
Place margarine in medium microwave-safe dish; cook on High power for 30 seconds. Add vegetables; cook on High power about 2 to 3 minutes, or until tender. Add eggs; cook on High power about 1 to 2 minutes, or until eggs are almost set. Rotate pan; stir in hot dog slices. Microwave for 30 seconds, or until hot dogs are heated through. Stir to break up eggs. Add cheese and cook on Medium power (50%)

about 10 to 15 seconds, or until cheese is melted. Garnish as above.

NUTRITION INFORMATION PER SERVING:
272 calories, 13.1 g protein, 24 g fat, 3.1 g carbohydrates, 304 mg cholesterol, 347 mg sodium.

TOASTED BACON & CHEESE ROLL-UPS

Makes 2 to 4 servings

4 ounces light cream cheese,
   softened
4 tablespoons golden raisins,
   chopped
¼ teaspoon apple pie spice
4 slices whole wheat bread
4 slices Armour Lower Salt
   Bacon, cooked crisp and
   finely crumbled
1½ tablespoons unsalted
   margarine or butter,
   melted

Preheat oven to 350°F. Mix cream cheese, raisins and apple pie spice in small bowl; spread evenly on bread slices. Sprinkle evenly with bacon. Roll up bread slices and secure with wooden toothpicks; brush with margarine. Bake on cookie sheet about 6 to 8 minutes, or until crisp and brown. If desired, sprinkle with shredded lower salt cheese and continue baking until cheese is melted.

NUTRITION INFORMATION PER SERVING:
233 calories, 8.4 g protein, 14.6 g fat, 20 g carbohydrates, 30.7 mg cholesterol, 401 mg sodium.

Left: Cheesy Vegetable Scrambled Eggs; right: Toasted Bacon & Cheese Roll-Ups

MAC & CHEESE DOGS

Makes 2 servings

½ cup uncooked corkscrew
    pasta, cooked according to
    package directions
    omitting salt and drained
¼ cup evaporated skim milk
¼ cup (1 ounce) shredded
    Armour Lower Salt
    Cheddar Cheese
½ teaspoon chili powder
2 Armour Lower Salt Jumbo
    Meat Hot Dogs
1 (6-inch) pita bread, cut in
    half
1 green onion, thinly sliced

Keep cooked pasta warm. Heat milk in small saucepan over medium-high heat; add cheese and chili powder. Cook for 5 minutes, or until cheese is melted. Stir in pasta; keep warm. Place hot dogs in small saucepan of boiling water. Cover and turn off heat. Let stand for 7 minutes. Slice hot dogs; add to pasta mixture. Spoon into pita halves; top with green onion, if desired.

MICROWAVE DIRECTIONS:
Keep cooked pasta warm. Heat milk in large microwave-safe pan on High power about 2 to 3 minutes, or until hot. Add cheese and chili powder; cook on High power about 2 to 3 minutes, or until cheese is melted. Stir in pasta; mix well. Wrap each hot dog in paper towel; cook on High power about 45 seconds to 1 minute, or until heated through.

Slice hot dogs; add to pasta mixture. Spoon into pita halves; top with green onion, if desired.

NUTRITION INFORMATION PER SERVING: 374 calories, 17.1 g protein, 20.7 g fat, 30.3 g carbohydrates, 46.2 mg cholesterol, 699 mg sodium.

BACON & CHICKEN SANDWICHES

Makes 3 servings

1 (5-ounce) can cooked white
    meat chicken, drained
1 small stalk celery, thinly
    sliced
1 green onion, sliced
½ cup plain nonfat yogurt
    Pepper to taste
3 hamburger buns, toasted
3 canned pineapple rings,
    well drained
3 slices Armour Lower Salt
    Bacon, cooked crisp and
    crumbled

Combine chicken, celery, onion, yogurt and pepper in small bowl. If desired, place lettuce leaf on bottom of each bun; place pineapple ring on lettuce. Top each with one third of the chicken mixture and bacon.

NUTRITION INFORMATION PER SERVING: 268 calories, 18.6 g protein, 5.7 g fat, 33.2 g carbohydrates, 40 mg cholesterol, 567 mg sodium.

*Top: Mac & Cheese Dogs;
bottom: Bacon & Chicken Sandwiches*

NUTRITION INFORMATION

	Calories (Kcal)	Protein (g)	Fat (g)	Carbohydrates (g)	Sodium (mg)	Cholesterol (mg)
BACON cooked—per 0.2 ounce (6 g) slice						
Armour Lower Salt Bacon, cooked	30	2.1	2.4	trace	126	6.0
Armour Star Bacon, cooked	31	2.1	2.5	trace	188	6.0
HAM cooked—per 1 ounce (28 g) slice						
Armour Lower Salt Ham 93% Fat Free	41	5.1	1.4	0.4	240	14.0
Armour Star Speedy Cut Ham	44	4.5	2.6	0.4	330	14.0
JUMBO HOT DOGS per 2 ounce (57 g) hot dog						
Armour Lower Salt Jumbo Hot Dog	170	7	15	2.0	450	30.0
Armour Star Jumbo Hot Dog	190	6	18	2.0	562	30.0
JUMBO BEEF HOT DOGS per 2 ounce (57 g) hot dog						
Armour Lower Salt Jumbo Beef Hot Dog	170	7	15	2.0	440	30.0
Armour Star Jumbo Beef Hot Dog	190	6	18	2.0	562	30.0
CHEESE* per 1 ounce (28 g) slice						
Armour Lower Salt Colby Cheese	110	7	9	1.0	120	30.0
Armour Lower Salt Monterey Jack Cheese	110	7	9	1.0	111	30.0
Armour Lower Salt Cheddar Cheese	110	7	9	1.0	106	30.0

*Regular Colby cheese has an average of 170 mg of sodium per ounce. Regular Monterey Jack cheese has an average of 160 mg of sodium per ounce. Regular Cheddar cheese has an average of 180 mg of sodium per ounce.

INDEX

Maia Whitehead

SHADE'S
Forest

Maia Whitehead

READYAIMWRITE
kids

READYAIMWRITE
k!ds

Shade's Forest

Maia Whitehead
Copyedited and typeset by Rebecca Millen

www.KidsWriteStories.net

First U.S. Edition, 2023-05-01

ISBN: 979-8-9875194-3-1

Printed in the U.S.A.

This book is dedicated to my mom and dad. You're the best parents in the whole world.
And to Hammy. You were always a wild child, and I wish you had been able to be with me for longer.

Table of Contents

Prologue

SHADE'S
Forest

Prologue

Shade awoke to the sound of whispered mews. It was still pitch dark out. Groggily, she opened her eyes. Snatches of conversation floated through her ears.

"When will you come back... the kittens..."

"You'll come later... Lilac...no..."

"I'll miss you, Beast."

She sat up. What was going on? Was Father leaving?

"Mother, what's happening?" she asked. Suddenly she was wide awake.

"Shade, I'm sorry we haven't told you." It was her father, Beast, who answered.

"Your father has decided to leave our owner's home. When you and your siblings are older, we will come to find him," her mother explained.

"But why? Why must he leave? Why, Father?"

"Hush, Shade, hush. One day you'll understand. I'll explain it all in due time. But you can't say a word to Thunder or Rose, got it?"

"Yes."

"Now, go to sleep."

Shade had a hard time falling asleep. She went to her bed and curled up with her siblings, but she couldn't help but watch as her father slipped out of a slightly open window and into the night. She couldn't stop thinking about what would happen if he got hurt out there, or if they couldn't find him, or if they would ever see him again.

Chapter One
Leaving

Shade flew through the air, hard on the tail of her brother, Thunder, while her sister, Rose, scampered alongside her. She squealed with excitement as Thunder rounded a corner, sprinting up the stairs of their small cabin in Pine Grove Forest. He suddenly leaped high into the air, skidding to a halt and sending his sisters crashing into him. He hissed mischievously and leaped upon Shade, pinning her down as she tried to dash away. He tickled her nose with his whiskers, and she purred with pleasure in spite of herself. She writhed under his grasp, but not as hard as she could have. Finally, she could take it no longer. Using all the strength and agility she could muster, she turned on her back and sprang into the air, twisting as she landed to face her bigger, but not older, brother. Now that she was three months old, she could pull off these moves with ease. Just behind him, she could see Rose sneaking up. The look of shock and surprise on Thunder's face when Rose leapt on him was priceless.

Just then, their mother, Lilac, walked into the room. She purred in amusement at the way

Thunder, Rose, and Shade froze all at once, staring at her. They relaxed at the look of affection in her eyes when she saw them, and Thunder instantly began to complain.

"Mother, look what they're doing to me! I was just getting something to eat when they started to chase me!"

"No, you tried to steal my food!" Rose protested.

"I was just helping Rose," Shade explained. "She was eating at one of the bowls, the one with the fish on it, because the other one was empty. Then Thunder came in and said that the bowl was his. He tried to steal it from her!"

"I did not!" Thunder argued, looking pleadingly at Lilac.

"It's okay, kittens, no one's in trouble," she said. "I just came in to show you something." There was a soft, almost melancholy tone to her voice. She led them down the stairs, through the hall, and into the living room. She helped them clamber onto a large, overstuffed couch that had its back to the window. The kittens clawed their way up the back, while their mother leapt with ease up onto the windowsill.

From here, they could see the woods spread out before them. The afternoon sun dappled the forest floor a thousand shades of green, while the branches swayed in the wind. The forest itself seemed to be alive with small creatures skittering about and colorful birds that swooped overhead. Shade felt an instant pulling to the woods, like it was out there in the forest that she belonged, not in this tiny cabin. Lilac's voice brought her back to reality.

"Get comfortable, kittens, we'll be here a while. I'm going to tell you a story. When you were only five weeks old, your father, Beast, left for the forest. I promised him that we'd be together. And now I believe you're ready."

As she talked, an old memory sparked inside of Shade. She remembered waking up to the sound of whispering. Remembered her mother explaining what was happening. Remembered the feeling of loss she had felt, for just a moment, when he left. And for the first time in a long time, she looked back on what it was like to have two parents. To have the gentle care and understanding of a mother and the confidence and support of a father. Her thoughts drifted back to the present, and she heard her mother speaking.

"We'll leave soon, in the late summer. I'll make sure to scout out an open window or something we can escape through. Your father will be waiting for us on the other side of the road. But once we're out, we'll have to travel a long way. It will take at least two d-"

Thunder interrupted, his eyes wide with fright. "But what if we get lost? Or what if a nasty fox finds us? Or what if we can never find Father?"

"Thunder, calm down," she said soothingly.

"I know the way in this forest. Your father said that he'd leave his scent trail, and the foxes only come out at night. Hopefully we won't be out then."

This time it was Shade who spoke. "Where will we go? Isn't it dangerous out there?"

"It's going to be fine, and I'll be with you every step of the way. Time for your nap. And remember, I will never leave your side."

The setting sun cast a red glow into the window, silhouetting the four cats against it, and Shade knew that her mother's words were true.

Shade blinked open her eyes. Thunder and Rose were already awake, even though it was dark out. Lilac was going over the plan of how to escape. Excitement started coursing through her. With her adrenaline rushing high, she rose onto her feet and walked over to her mother. She had just finished going over the fact that they would have to cross a very busy, very dangerous road.

"Are we ready?" her mother asked solemnly.

"Yes," they chorused.

Lilac, Thunder, Rose, and Shade leapt onto the couch that they had surveyed the woods from the day before and slipped through the open window into the dark night. As her eyes adjusted to the dim moonlight, Shade began to look around. Behind them was the log cabin she had spent all her life in, and to the left was the small tool shed. But it was where they were facing that intrigued her. The woods. They looked very different at night. The trees were dark silhouettes against the full moon, and instead of birdsong, she heard the chirping of crickets and the rustling of leaves in the wind. Suddenly, a shriek ripped through the air. It sounded like a human scream, combined with the howl of a wounded animal. Lilac froze, tense.

"Fox," she whispered, her eyes darting around. The scream came again, followed by a series of high-pitched yips. "Follow me, stay close and don't. Make. A. Sound."

Trembling with fright, Shade and her siblings followed Lilac as she crept alongside the cabin, keeping close to its side. They finally got to the tool shed after what felt like ages. Fur bristling, they squeezed through a gap in the door and walked towards the middle of the shed. It was crowded with various types of tools. A lawn mower sat unused in the back, and several rakes leaned against the walls, cobwebs draping over the handles.

"If the fox catches our scent, he hopefully won't be able to follow," said Lilac. Shade didn't have time to ask how she knew it was a male as their mother led them to the back of the shed. There, she caught sight of a low shelf, then another, then another, and finally a small loft that towered above their heads, close to the ceiling.

"Follow me," Lilac mewed. They leaped from shelf to shelf until they got to the loft. Out of breath, Shade sank to the floor and curled up with Thunder and Rose while Lilac kept watch. Gradually, she fell into an uneasy sleep, full of visions of teeth slashing and foxes hunting them down.

In the early morning, just before dawn, Lilac woke them. Stomachs growling and limbs aching from the hard surface they'd slept on, they clambered down from the wooden shelves.

"It's time to get going," Lilac said.

"But what about the fox?" asked Rose worriedly.

"It's gone."

Once more, they squeezed through the opening and into the fresh air. Shade could just see the sun peeking out from behind the trees as they hurried into the forest. Memories from the fox incident the night before made the fur on the back of her neck rise, and she hurried to catch up with Lilac and her siblings. The forest seemed so much bigger than when she'd seen it through the window. The trees grew as tall as the roof of the cabin, even taller. Their bright green leaves rustled in the gentle breeze, but Shade could already sense that fall was coming. The sun was rising slowly, and it spilled light over the treetops, dappling the forest floor and giving light to the many bushes and ferns that covered the ground. *It's beautiful*, she thought. She felt like she could spend her entire life here. It was as if the woods went on forever.

"Does it go on forever?" Rose asked in awe, voicing Shade's exact thoughts.

"No," Lilac answered with a laugh. "But it is big."

Shade looked around her again. *That's for sure,* she thought. It was midday before Lilac called a halt. Thunder had been grumbling and complaining for the last hour about how tired he was, but however annoying it was, Shade couldn't help but silently agree. Her paws ached from walking so far, and her eyelids drooped under the hot and dreary sunlight.

"We'll take a break and shelter under this

bush until tomorrow," Lilac announced. Shade sighed with relief, and Thunder immediately flopped down under the bush. Shade followed his lead, and began grooming her legs. Bits of dead leaves and dirt had gotten stuck and mangled in her black fur, even though she was a shorthair. Despite her sibling's obvious exhaustion, Rose stood beside the low hanging bush, showing no signs of tiredness at all.

"Aren't you going to rest?" Thunder asked in surprise.

"Maybe," replied Rose. "I'm just so excited about seeing Father again that I can't wait to keep going," she explained, bouncing energetically on her toes.

"Oh," said Thunder and Shade together.

Shade was a little bit startled that Rose even remembered their father and suddenly wondered if Rose had been missing him all of the time he was gone. But she didn't ask. If Rose had wanted to talk about their father, she would have already brought it up.

After a while, Thunder, Shade, and even Rose had fallen asleep, but now it was the next day, and all three were eager to get going. They ran ahead of Lilac, scampering around and hiding in the bushes. Rose chased her siblings around in a circle, dead leaves fluttering in the wind they created in their frenzied dash. Eventually, Shade noticed a distant roaring, and an acrid tang began tinting the pine smelling air. Up ahead, she could see a break in the tree line, like there was some kind of river or something. As they approached, the roaring grew louder, and Shade realized what it was. *This must be the road Mother was talking about,* she thought. She was filled with excitement, and she pricked her ears nervously. The roaring sound was now deafening, and the smell so strong she could hardly bear it. Still, they crept closer. When they were only a few feet away, Lilac stopped them.

"Now listen," she said. "This is the road. You may look at it, but you must not set a paw on it. It could cost you your life."

Cautiously, they stalked closer. Shade peered through the thick shrubs and gasped. What she saw was a great black river, completely solid, with huge monsters rushing past. The powerful wind blew back her whiskers and ruffled her fur. Scared, she took a step back, bumping into Thunder.

"Watch it!" he said indignantly.

"Sorry," she apologized. She walked back to Lilac on trembling legs.

"Do we have to cross it?" she asked shakily.

"Yes, but we'll cross when it's less busy. Right now, I've got to hunt. Tell Thunder and Rose where I am."

When Lilac came back, her jaws were loaded with three small, grayish brown, furry creatures. Shade could smell them before her mother was even in sight.

"What *are* those?" She was intrigued and

curious about their delicious and warm scent. Lilac dropped them onto the ground.

"It's mouse. Take a small bite, see if you like it."

Shade bent down and closed her teeth around the mouse. A warm, rich, and salty flavor filled her mouth. Eagerly, she took another bite, then another, until the whole thing was gone, leaving only a few wisps of fur and a patch of blood on the ground. Licking her lips, she turned to see that Thunder and Rose had come back from where they had been playing together.

"Look what Mother brought!" she exclaimed. "It's called mouse, and it's the most delicious thing I've ever tasted. I've never had anything like it. Try it, try it!"

Thunder scampered over to one of the mice, while Rose warily sniffed at the other before trying it. Thunder's was gone in moments, and he immediately tried to swipe Rose's. She hissed and he backed off, looking hungrily at the one she was still finishing.

"Is there more?" he asked hopefully.

"No, Thunder, but you'll have some for dinner," said Lilac, a twinkle in her eye.

Shade walked over to a thick bush and lay down alongside Thunder and Rose beneath the shrub they had chosen. She absentmindedly began grooming Rose between the ears, while she and Thunder licked each other. With the midmorning sun shining over the treetops and

19

her head full of thoughts of the day before and what they were going to do next, she fell asleep. Lilac woke them when the sun was at its highest. Shade lifted her head, leaving the peace of sleep behind as she rose.

"It's time to go," said Lilac softly. She walked to the road, looking over her shoulder to make sure they were following. Once more, the tang of the street filled Shade's nose, and she wrinkled it to drive out the smell. As the road came into view, a sudden fear filled her, and her belly tightened up. She glanced anxiously at her mother for directions. Lilac turned, and seeing her worried face, she said, "We'll cross one at a time. I'll go with Rose, then Thunder. You can go last to see how we do it. Don't worry my love, we'll be okay."

Lilac faced Rose. Shade hadn't realized how scared she was. She was trembling, and her voice shook as she said goodbye to her and Thunder. Lilac licked her comfortingly on the head and murmured something to her. They walked back to the edge of the road, Rose looking anxiously back at her siblings. Shade gave her an encouraging nod, and Thunder purred. Staring back at the bustling street once more, Rose pressed against Lilac's side.

"I'm ready," she whispered to her mother.

Searching for a gap in the cars, Lilac shouted, "Now!" She and Rose sped off across the street, and soon they were hidden from view by the seemingly endless stream of trucks

and cars. Shade and Thunder waited nervously
on the other side until they could make out
Lilac sprinting across.

"You're back! Is Rose okay?" Shade asked,
as she ran to meet her mother.

"She's okay," Lilac said, then turned her
attention to Thunder. He looked at her
fearfully. "Are you ready? Do exactly what
Rose and I did, alright?"

"Alright," Thunder gulped. He gave Shade a
brief lick on the top of the head, and then they
were gone. Shade caught a glimpse of them
leaping away from the traffic into the bushes
on the other side. Relieved, she sat and waited.
As Lilac reached her, all the nerves and terror
at crossing suddenly came back to her. Wide-

eyed and shaking, she backed away.

"No, Mother, no! I-I can't do this!" she whimpered. She crouched, the unexpected weight of all that had happened dropping down on her. But Lilac gently grasped her scruff, tugging her back into view of the road. She groomed her all over, licking stray tufts of fur back in place with loving care. Shade calmed.

"Come. Your siblings will be worried about us," Lilac whispered softly, her voice full of affection. She nudged Shade forward. "And don't forget that I love you more than anything else in the world, and we will always be together. This road is only one of the many adventures you'll have." A serious tone entered her voice. "When I say go, you run. As fast as you can, as hard as you can, no matter what happens, all the way to the other side, do you understand?"

"Yes." All the shakiness had left Shade's body, and she found herself in a strange state of icy calm. She took a deep breath.

"Go!" Lilac howled.

Shade sprang into action. Legs pumping like pistons, she shot across the street. Just as she was nearing the end, a large, black car sped towards them. Time seemed to stop. Her eyes watered from the wind. Lilac slowed, putting herself between the car and Shade. Lilac screeched in agony as the vehicle slammed into her body at full force, throwing her to the side, the huge, black tires crushing the tip of her tail.

Shade panicked and spun around, dashing back the way she'd come. She yowled in terror as another car drove past, and she leapt over her mother's body, splashing her front paws in a pool of crimson, red blood. She made it to the other side and glimpsed Rose dashing into the woods on the other side, wailing, while Thunder stood stock still, eyes wide open and staring at the spot where Lilac had stood just moments before. The setting sun's rays cast a bloodred light over the whole scene, reminding Shade of the puddle of it drying on the road.

Finally, Shade could bear it no longer. She turned her head away from the road, away from the smell of death, the feeling of loss, and the furry lump that was once her wonderful,

wonderful mother.

Shade crouched behind a screen of bushes, grief racking her body as she watched the sun set over the forest. She peered through the branches at her mother's body, and her heart ached, thinking of all the amazing things her mother had done for her, all the times she had explained something difficult, stopped a fight with her siblings, calmed her after a nightmare, or shared her food when the other bowls were empty. Shade realized that she would never again have that motherly kind of love, and that if she followed through and buried her, she would never see her again.

As soon as the sun slipped behind the mountains and the traffic thinned, she got up and crept onto the road. Checking for cars, she walked up to her mother. Her body was already cold. She shuddered and stared hard across the street, but Thunder and Rose had both disappeared into the woods on the other side. Giving up, she bent and sniffed Lilac's pelt.

Deep beneath the stench of death and the sharp, smoky edge of the road, there was a warm, milky, sweet scent. The scent of her mother. She grasped Lilac's scruff, gently but firmly, and dragged her to the bush where Shade had rested. Letting her jaws rest, she laid her mother on the ground beside the bush. Then she began grooming her. She moved her tongue in long strokes, starting at the shoulders and moving down. When she got to the base of her tail, she went up to her head. She used hard, fast licks to smooth her fur out. When she finished, she curled up next to her mother like she had so many times in the past, and fell asleep.

Overnight, her mother had turned from a beautiful Bengal to a lifeless, cold shape of a cat. Anguished to see her that way, Shade immediately started to search for an appropriate burial site. She found a small clearing, sheltered on one side by laurels and pine trees, and on the other, a wall of seemingly solid underbrush. Soft grass covered the site, and she began to dig. She first ripped up a circle of grass the size of Lilac.

Unsheathing her claws, she tore at the

ground until it was several feet deep. Claws aching, but feeling that it was the right decision, she made her way back to the street. Once more she took her mother by the scruff and carried her to the grave. Lowering her in, she arranged her so that she looked as if she was sleeping. She found a single lilac bush growing on its own at the edge of the clearing. She nipped off a clump of the sweet-smelling flowers and laid it on her side. Slipping a paw over Lilac's eyes, she filled in the grave. And though the hole in the ground was full, it had created an even bigger hole in her heart.

Chapter Two

Mourning

Memories from the night before created nightmares in Shade's dream world. She dreamt that she had crossed the road with her mother, just like in reality. But when she went to sleep with Lilac, she had woken up to find her mother standing over her, baring her teeth. *But she's dead*, she thought, cold dread beginning to creep through her. Looking down, Shade saw a fresh wound on her shoulder. The flesh around the area was rotting away. As she lifted her head, she saw her mother sprinting off into the dark, misty forest.

Shade woke with a start, eyes wide. She stared around, her heart pounding and her fur bristling. As the fear and horror of the dream faded, she sat up, finding herself on the edge of the clearing where she'd buried Lilac. The events of the day before and the harsh feeling of loss had taken their toll on her body, and she'd fallen asleep at the site out of pure exhaustion.

Blinking her eyes in the dim light of dawn, she realized that she would have to choose whether she would go back and try to find her owner's home or once more attempt to cross the street and hope to find her siblings. She no longer knew the way back to her owner's house, and fear prevented her from even thinking about going back to the place where her mother had died. The only sensible thing to do now was to head into the woods. Head into the woods where there were foxes and snakes, and she had no idea how to hunt, and where winter came cold and bitter. She scoffed at the thought. But there was nothing else she could do.

As Shade started off, the first thing that came to her mind was the desperate need for food that lingered in her stomach. She hadn't eaten since Lilac had caught their food the day after they escaped. Her belly rumbled at the thought of the delicious meat she'd tasted that her mother said was mouse, but she didn't know how to hunt, let alone teach herself without guidance.

Shade wandered the forest, shocked and numb from the bitter experience. Her stomach twisted in pain from being empty for so long, reminding her that she would have to figure it out eventually. Feeling as if she was about to pass out, hunger gnawed at her insides, and her instincts kicked in. She sniffed the air and detected a faint scent of mouse. She crept towards the smell, and she could feel the pulse of a tiny heart beating as it reached her paws through the ground. As the scent grew stronger, she realized that it was not a mouse she had found. Peering through the bushes, she sighted a small, rusty orange colored creature, with three black stripes running down its back. Its tail was darker than the rest of its body, and it had beady black eyes that darted around as it nibbled on a nut. It reminded her of the animals she'd seen running about on the first day her mother had shown her the forest.

Slowly, she crept further. Still unaware of her, it dropped its nut and scrambled onto a log, letting out a series of high-pitched chirps. Her eyes quickly followed it. She decided that even if it wasn't a mouse, she could at least try to eat it. Carefully, she put one paw in front of another, her belly fur scraping gently against the dead leaves. She held her breath as one crunched beneath her paw. The creature ignored her. She was glad of the thick shrubbery to hide her midnight black pelt. After what felt like hours, she was close enough to pounce. She bunched her muscles, getting ready to leap. With her haunches waving in the air, she sprang into the sky, flying several feet. She landed squarely on the little animal, pinning her thorn sharp claws on its back.

It squealed in terror, and Shade's heart lurched. It reminded her of the agonized screech Lilac had let out just before she was killed. Shaking off the feeling, she bent down and instinctively nipped the animal on the back of the neck. As the feeling of pride at her first catch faded, she saw that it was a juvenile, and a puny one at that. She gobbled it down in only a couple bites. Her stomach calmed, but it was barely halfway full.

Shade looked up at the sky to see that the sun was almost setting. She realized that she would have to find shelter. It was not as warm as it used to be, and some of the trees were already dropping leaves, not to mention the foxes that she was sure were out there. She turned around, wondering where she should search first. Spotting a patch of trees that were knitted unusually close together, she headed towards them, figuring that she could at least hide in the thicket.

The sun was rapidly setting, and she picked

up the pace. After a few minutes of searching, she spotted a seemingly worthy place to rest. It was a dense clump of ferns, and, looking closer, in the middle of the small patch of ferns was a boulder. Curious, she walked around it until she noticed a thinning in the plants. Squeezing through the narrow opening, she crept along the tunnel of ferns. As the boulder up ahead became easier to see, she also could pick out an area of rock that was eroded away. Still crouched down, she worked her way through the foliage to the stone. As she stood, she found that she could easily fit in the rundown hollow of the rock. Pleased, she made a mental note on where the exact location was, knowing she would explore more the next day.

Once more her stomach growled, ruining her pleasant mood. Grumpily, she decided that the best way to silence it was to go to sleep.

When she woke up, she was hungrier than ever. She sat up, shaking dirt from her pelt. She blinked her eyes in the pale morning light and shivered. Nights had been getting colder. She walked out from under the rock and slipped through the fern tunnel. Stretching, she breathed in the crisp morning air, glad that she was alive. It pained her to think of who wasn't. Taking her mind off of it, she returned to the task at hand – hunting. She struggled to catch even the faintest scent of prey in the air and began to walk through the forest. She had to search for several minutes before she could smell anything. It was a mouse, and this time she was sure of it. She followed the scent. As Shade drew closer, she could hear it scrabbling about in the low-growing vegetation. She stalked carefully forward until it came into view. Luckily, it seemed to be larger than the mouse Lilac had brought back and was quite plump.

Trying a different method than the day before, Shade came as close as possible to her prey before she shot out a paw, claws outstretched. It missed by mere inches, but before the mouse could escape, she launched herself after it. Clamping her paw around its body, she killed it swiftly and took a bite. It was the best she'd ever tasted, better even

than the mouse Lilac had caught for her.
Licking her lips, she savored the delicious
flavor and tenderness of the meat. When she
was done, she buried the few bones left. She
didn't want to attract unwelcome predators by
leaving the scent and bones lying around.

Looking around, she suddenly felt the need
to explore. To see *all* of her new territory.
Perhaps she would even find her owner's
house. But a tiny voice in her head told her that
even though there was a chance she might find
the old log cabin, she could never go back to
that lifestyle. Her whole life she had longed to
go out into the woods. Now she had the
chance. Now she was a wild cat. Now, she was
free.

Shade set off towards the direction of her den. She walked past it, knowing that she could never miss the big clump of trees that it was hidden in. After traveling for some time, she became aware of her thirst. Her tongue felt dry, and her mouth had a bitter taste to it. She steadied onwards, hoping to find a stream, or even a small puddle. At last, she sighted one. It was a shallow puddle, and the water was murky and muddy, but she drank deeply anyway. As she continued, she noticed a distant sound. It reminded her of the road, but there was no smell. Cautiously, she crept closer. Through a gap in the trees, light glinted off of something, shining brightly through the branches of the trees. The sound came closer.

Shade realized what it was. *Water*, she thought. *Running water!*

She bounded forward. Back at the cabin she and her siblings had had a special water bowl. It had a tiny little waterfall that trickled water into the main bowl. She used to splash Thunder and Rose with it. What she now saw before her was like that, except huge. It wound its way through the forest just like the road had, and the rushing water burbled and shone in the sunlight. Purring, she ran up to it. She lowered her muzzle gratefully into the stream and drank her fill.

Afterwards, she lightly dipped her paws in. She'd never been afraid of getting wet like her siblings, and the cool water was soothing on her aching paw pads. Satisfied with her discovery, she headed back to her den. She arrived exhausted but pleased, her eyelids drooping. The sun was setting, and she realized how long she had been out. From the safety of her den, she watched it set, marveling at the beautiful hues of pink, orange, red, and blue. She slipped into a peaceful sleep.

Shade rose from her den full of energy, longing to explore more of her territory and wanting to go back to the stream. She stretched luxuriously and flexed her muscles. Knowing that she would have to hunt before setting off again, she tracked her prey close to the road. But this time it was neither a mouse, nor one of the small, rusty colored animals she'd hunted.

This one was a medium sized mammal, a light gray in color, with a bushy tail. Her mother had once told her that it was called a squirrel.

She had no objection to trying new things, so she stalked up to it. It had a distinct smell, like oak trees in the fall and dead leaves. Not letting this deter her, she crept onwards. Suddenly, it turned its head. Ears perked, it dropped the acorn it had been busy burying. Shade froze. Its eyes scanned the bushes where she hid. At last, it found her. Their eyes locked, and it bolted. With lightning reflexes, she tore after it. It made for the closest tree, but Shade was gaining, bit by bit. Just then, it leapt. Flying through the air, it landed on the trunk and shot up. Still, she didn't give up. Jumping after it, she followed it, clumsily rushing up the tree. Finally, she stretched a paw as far and fast as it would go towards the creature, at the same time pushing off with her back legs. The tip of her claw caught in its thick tail fur, and she yanked it down. It squealed, but it was too late. She jumped down from the tree with her prize in her mouth. She ate it slowly, panting from the chase. She shook out her fur, savoring victory. *Time to explore,* she thought. Even though her limbs ached, she was eager to see what else was in store for her in this wilderness.

She walked in the opposite direction as the day before. Strolling about, she relished the feel of the early morning sun soaking through her fur. She had started to grow her winter coat, and although the thicker layer on her body kept her relatively warm, it was nice to feel the sun on her skin again.

Shade marveled at the fall colors that were beginning to seep into the flora around her. There was a light breeze stirring the branches covered in pale green, yellow, orange, and red leaves around her. A sudden happiness filled her, and she bounded forward, the wind rushing through her fur. She let out a caterwaul of pure joy.

As she slowed to a walk, she noticed that the woods around her had thinned. Shade was no longer in the thicket. A feeling of uneasiness swept over her, like deja-vu. Just then, she saw a clearing, and she realized where she was. Home, the cabin, the place where she had spent all of her days until now. She shivered and walked closer. It was just how they'd left it. The dark tiled roof, brown log walls, and the little tool shed they had sheltered from all those days ago were exactly the same. But strangely, it didn't make her sad to see the cabin again. Sure, she missed Thunder and Rose, and was still mourning for Lilac, but it made her grateful for the freedom she now had. When she was younger, the woods both intrigued and scared her, but now she was glad that she had left. The smell of the wind, the taste of prey, and the freedom of the entire forest at her paws was better than any cabin, no matter how cozy.

Turning around to leave, she thought about the fox that they had heard. *If it ever comes back,* she thought, *I've got to be ready.* She tried to come up with things she could do to ward it off if it ever did come back. The first thing that popped into her head was instinctual. She would mark her territory. Wondering where exactly her "territory" started and ended, she decided that it would definitely include part of the stream, and the shed of her owner's cabin.

She walked over to the cabin and lifted a leg to spray. A small amount came out, and she did it again on a tree nearby. She bounded a couple yards towards her thicket and sprayed once more. She made her way all the way to the stream, where she stopped. She walked along it for a considerable distance before looping back around to the tool shed. By then the sun was setting, and Shade was tired. It had been a long trek, and she wondered if it had been the wrong thing to do. What if her scent attracted the fox instead of repelling it? She didn't want to think about what would happen if it did come, but the thought lingered in the back of her mind as she walked back to her den. Just to be safe, she gathered a few twigs and branches and built a partial wall around the entrance to her den, making it even more narrow. Feeling a little bit more secure, she slipped inside and fell asleep.

When Shade woke up, she was *cold*. That

night had been extremely frigid, for an autumn night, and it forced her to think about what she would do when winter time came. A chill ran down her spine, and she curled into a tight ball, hoping to conserve her body heat. She closed her eyes and tried to fall asleep just so she could wake up when it was warmer, but it was so cold that she couldn't. She got up and stretched, then she walked down the tunnel.

It was colder out here than in her den, and she began to shiver. Still, she made herself search for prey. Just when she thought that all of the little animals that she hunted were still hiding in their burrows and nests, she spotted a mouse. She was hungry, though not as much as before. She stalked towards it, carefully placing one paw in front of the other. She kept her eyes on her prey, not wanting to miss it. At last, she leapt. She landed right on it, with her claws digging into its skin. She bent down and killed it, then took a bite. She ate slowly, savoring the flavor. Finishing it off, she stood.

By then it was mid-morning, and she had warmed up a little. Not knowing what to do next and feeling kind of bored, Shade wandered back to her den. Looking at it from the outside, she noticed that some of the ferns sheltering the boulder had withered a bit in the cold. She thought that it would probably be useful to have a little more protection against the freezing weather, and maybe foxes. First, she gathered a few medium sized branches and lots of small sticks and dead leaves. She carried the branches to the boulder and leaned them up against it, leaving a small gap for her to go in and out of. Next, she grabbed mouthfuls of the small twigs. She bent and weaved them in between the larger sticks until it formed a patchwork of wood. For insulation, Shade jammed the dead leaves onto the inside and outside of the wall. When she was done, it looked pretty secure from the freezing wind outside. Glad she had finished before night, she crept inside. Even though the sun was still out, it felt good to rest, knowing she would be better protected from the cold and potential predators.

Chapter Three

Storm

The stream burbled as Shade walked along it. It was warmer than the day before, a good day to patrol her territory. She paused to take a quick drink, the cool water soothing her dry throat. She continued on her way, the loop of her territory almost done. She had decided that it was a good idea to patrol her territory every day, or every other day, and she had just passed the shed. She'd found out that it was a good place to hunt, and she had eaten a feast of a mouse and one of the gray, bushy tailed creatures, a squirrel. She was feeling like she had become quite a hunter.

Happiness and contentment filled her, and she leaped into a pile of red and orange leaves, spraying them all around her. She squealed and jumped up, batting at them with her paws. She caught one in her mouth and looked around as if someone were there to see her skills. A wave of sadness caught her by surprise. She wished that Thunder and Rose were there to play with her, and her mother there to be impressed by her quick reflexes. She let go of the leaf in her mouth and slowly walked away, her head down. She didn't want to think about it.

As she trudged through the dense undergrowth towards her den, she realized that she was still a young cat, no more than three months old. No matter how good at hunting she was, or how brave she was at the moment, she would have to grow up, at least in maturity. She sighed as she neared the den, recognizing hunger once more. She would have to hunt again.

The squirrel escaped up into the branches of the tree above. Shade cursed under her breath. She stood on the roots of the tree, panting. The first time she'd caught a squirrel, the momentum from her run had gotten her far enough up the tree to catch it, but this time, it was too close to the tree for her to follow.

Disappointed, she settled for mouse. She had developed a taste for squirrels, and ate them as often as she could. But the mouse would have to do. She searched for a while before she scented anything, then saw a mouse under a tree, nibbling on something in its paws. She was already close enough to catch it, and she pounced. She killed it quickly and ate.

As she walked back to the maple tree that the squirrel had escaped up into, an idea sparked in her head. What if *she* learned how to climb? Then she could follow the squirrels up, and she could leap down from the branches onto prey. The idea grew in her mind until she knew she had to try. Determination filled her, and she took off in search of a good tree to practice on.

She came to the edge of her territory and looked around. Just as she'd expected, there was a huge tree, a pine, right at the edge, close to the tool shed. It towered above the other trees, its broad branches spreading out over the cabin. It had thick bark as well, perfect for digging in her claws. Shade knew exactly where to start.

Walking back a few yards, she took off to a running start, building speed. When she was about two feet away from the tree trunk, she pushed off with her hind legs, landing on the trunk. She gripped it with unsheathed claws, exerting all of her strength in her limbs. She made it up several feet, but was forced to let go. Dropping to the ground, she took a moment before trying again.

This time, she tried a different strategy. She went to the base of the tree, stretching her claws out as far as they would go, and put her front paws on the bark, digging them in. She placed her back paws on the tree. Now all four of her paws were on the trunk. She carefully moved her front paws up, one at a time. She had almost gone to the first branch when a strip of bark peeled from beneath her paw. Her claws slipped from their hold and she fell backwards. She twisted in midair, landing with a thud on the forest floor. Stunned, she staggered to her feet, panting.

She shook her head to clear it and tried

again. She padded over to the pine, extending her claws. She took her front paws and reached up as far as they would go, then put her back legs on the trunk as well. She dug in her claws and cautiously slid her front paws up. She did the same with her back paws, and kept doing it, faster than earlier, all the way to the first branch. She hauled herself on. Struggling to keep her balance, she crouched down. She had climbed, just like the squirrel!

As she found her footing, she looked around. The forest was spread out before her like a map. This first branch was high. So high, in fact, that she could see the tops of some of the smaller trees. She could see the roof of the tool shed below her, and the cabin in front. She had been so busy staring at the scenery beside her, she hadn't looked very closely at the forest floor. Now she could make out tiny little animals skittering about in the shrubbery. There was a mouse and several of the rusty colored creatures.

She breathed in the smells of the wood. Pine, leaves, and cool air. The wind blew, ruffling her fur. She stood up and decided that she was going to go higher. The second lowest branch was on the other side of the tree, and several feet above her. Taking the challenge, she leapt onto the trunk, latching on with all four sets of claws. She made her way sideways along the tree until she was directly under it, and started to clamber upward. Her right paw

found the base of the branch, and she pulled
herself up. This time, Shade didn't take the
time to observe the view. She paused just for a
moment to catch her breath, then continued.
There was a third bough about five feet above
her. She used the same strategy as the past few
branches and clawed her way up. She was
breathless by the time she got there, and she
took a minute to recover.

She looked up to scout out her next stop,
and saw the last thing she wanted to see when
she was thirty feet up in a pine tree. It was a
storm. And a big one. Shade scrambled about
the branch, trying to get down. She hooked her
claws in the bark and slid part ways down. She
landed heavily on the other branch, the breath

completely knocked out of her. She sat down and heard the first rumble of thunder. It spooked her, and she flinched. Almost losing her footing, she gripped it tighter.

The first drops of rain began to fall just then. In the beginning, it was just a light drizzle, but in seconds it had started pouring. Already drenched to the skin, Shade leapt from her perch. Landing on the first branch she'd climbed to, she didn't hesitate to jump again. As she landed, she slipped on the wet leaves. She scrambled onto her feet, sprinting in the direction of her den. The rain was coming down so hard she could barely see, and the thunder boomed as loudly as the road. Flashes of lighting lit up the sky, illuminating the ground as well. Finally, Shade sighted her den. Rushing inside, she shook as much of the water off as she could, wetting the walls of the den. Shaking, she laid down. With her eyes wide, she waited for the storm to pass.

Shade exhaled in relief. The storm had passed, and the sky was clear. She set out to hunt, hoping that the other animals would be out now that it wasn't raining. She hadn't gone far when she spotted a squirrel. Eager to use her new skills, she stalked closer. As soon as it caught sight of her, it ran. She bolted after it, but slowed down, letting it get a few feet up the tree before she followed. She clawed her way up, going as fast as she could.

The squirrel disappeared on the other side of

the tree. Moving as silently as possible, she climbed sideways. Her prey was looking the other way, and she shot out a paw. It grasped the squirrel from behind, yanking it down and into her jaws. She bit down on it, but it was already dead. Awkwardly, she twisted and jumped off of the tree. Pleased, but a bit embarrassed by her clumsy descent, she ate it quickly. Knowing that it would help her if she learned how to get down from the tree as well as up, she made her way back to the ancient pine she'd been practicing on before the storm. She hoped that it would be dry enough not to slip.

As she approached, she was glad to see that most of the rain had been deflected off by the other trees. The trunk looked a little moist, but dry enough. She pushed off the ground, and climbed up. She clawed her way onto the first branch. Without stopping to look at the view, she contemplated the best way to get down. She could always leap down, or slide, like she had in the storm, but it was easy for her to get hurt that way. She decided that the best way to go about it was to work her way down, tail first.

She now only unsheathed her front claws, leaving the back ones in. She latched her claws into the bark, swinging dangerously. She gripped the tree harder with her front paws, her back acting as support. Bracing herself with her claws, she carefully slid her back legs down about a foot. She unhooked one of her front paws, moving it down. She did this with each paw, interchanging them, until the ground was only a couple feet below her. She leaped down. The descent was smoother than earlier, and she felt a little bit of pride at her progress. She practiced for the rest of the day, enjoying the new skill she had. When she returned to her den, she laid down, resting her tired limbs and watching the sunset through the branches of the evergreens.

Chapter Four

Fear

When Shade woke up, the smell of fox was all around her. She recognized it from the night they escaped. Fear filled her to the brim. She leaped up, looking wildly about. She saw that the scent was from the night before, but it did nothing to calm her nerves. She crept out of the den, fur bristling. Tense, she wondered what to do next. She followed the scent trail a few feet before breaking off. She hadn't understood what would happen if she found it. She shuddered at the mere thought of facing an animal like that. She loped away to the left of the trail, heading towards the center of the thicket. Cautiously, she searched for her meal, seeing no point in going hungry while a fox was in the area. She ate quickly and moved on, searching for a safer place than her small den.

Just then, a screech sounded, ringing through the air. Shade jumped. Heart pounding, she realized that she was in danger. Grave danger. If the fox were to find her, it would all be over. She began to panic and sprinted in the opposite direction of the trail, hoping that it never knew she was there. Suddenly, the smell grew stronger. Shade froze. Leaves crunched

behind her. Her adrenaline was up and all of
her senses hyper. Remembering what her
mother had said about foxes not being able to
climb, she sprinted towards the nearest tree, the
pounding of paw steps following her. She shot
up, only stopping at the first branch. She
peered down, wide-eyed. The fox crashed
through the underbrush, oblivious of Shade's
hiding place and thinking that it was still on her
trail. She breathed a sigh of relief, closing her
eyes for a moment to steady her breathing.
Thinking about the fox that was probably still
out there, she climbed to the second branch,
then the third. She crouched trembling for a
while, her panic fading slowly. Still, she
dreaded having to come down from her hiding

place. Another shriek came, this time further away. She was reassured now that she knew the fox was gone.

But then, she heard another howl. Much closer. Where the first scent trail had been. With horror, she registered that it was at her den. She wouldn't be able to return. Surprised that her current home had meant so much to her, she couldn't help but feel a little sad that it was being destroyed. The fox had probably already ripped her wall to shreds because of her scent being layered so thickly inside. She thought about what to do next. She was going to have to eat at some point, but the thought of coming down terrified her. Once more a wail could be heard through the trees. Startled, she leapt up to the next branch. She was now almost half way up, and the forest floor seemed a hundred times smaller than usual. She kneaded the branch in distress, but there was nothing she could do about her treacherous situation.

She watched the sun rise higher and higher in the sky, a strange and unexpected loneliness settling inside of her. The whole ordeal would have been much easier if she'd just had Thunder and Rose beside her, or, even better, Lilac. She hung her head, overcome with sadness.

She decided that, just to be safe, she would stay in the tree until nighttime. Several hours had passed since the sun had set It was dark out, and the woods were silent. Unlike other nights, there were no crickets chirping, no owls hooting, just the wind rustling the leaves in the trees. The stench of fox was still heavy in the air, but Shade was starving. She hadn't eaten since breakfast the day before, but she was no less wary of the possible danger that lingered in the woods. She waited in the cold night air for some time before her desperate hunger drove her down.

Thanking her earlier self for learning to climb, she slid as silently as she could down the trunk, landing with a soft crunch on the dead leaves below. The eerie silence sent chills down her spine, and she looked watchfully around for any sign of her predator. Even though her stomach was growling madly, she knew that it would be a good idea to make sure that the fox was truly gone from the area before hunting, as she would be quite exposed while she ate. She crept around a large and thick bush, using her nose to search for anything that might tell her its location. Weaving her way in between the many trees, Shade followed the trail left from the day before.

Once more, the smell grew stronger. Knowing that the fox was still near, she detected another scent laid deep beneath the one of the fox – the warm odor of blood. It was fresh. She stood stock still, positive that the fox was right behind her. She heard a low growl. Turning slowly, she saw a pair of eyes glowing from in the dark in front of her. There was a long pause, Shade frozen in horror, the fox gradually creeping forward.

Shade backed off, the moments ticking away. Suddenly, it launched itself at her. Shade caught a glimpse of a foamy and blood-stained mouth with flashing eyes and thorn sharp teeth before she tore into the underbrush behind her. Limbs pumping as hard as she could make them, she shot into the dark forest. Eventually, the pounding of footfalls behind her subsided. In the distance, she heard a small yelp, and a thump. She had lost it.

Pondering about what had made it so savage, she looked around her. With surprise, she realized that she was back in the thicket. A few yards in front of her stood her den, the makeshift wall completely torn up. She saw that it would not be safe for her, and instead she climbed a very old tree nearby. Disturbed by what she had seen, she forgot all about her hunger as she clambered up. Never again would she look for foxes in the dead of night, she thought. She finally drifted into a restless sleep, wishing for all the world that she was back safe in the cabin with Thunder, Rose, and Lilac.

When Shade woke up, the hunger she felt was terrible. No matter how fearful she was about the fox, she had to hunt. She slid down from the tree. The scent of the foxes was fading slowly, and she felt more secure knowing that they weren't nearby. However, she had to travel a fair distance before she found an area where the prey hadn't been scared away. She tracked a mouse, finding the tiny creature crouched on the roots of a large, thick trunked tree. She pounced, catching it effortlessly.

Even after eating, she was still hungry. Searching once again for another meal, she spotted one of the rusty colored animals. Licking her lips, she crept towards it. She had developed a taste for them as well as squirrels, and she looked forward to eating it again, for she hadn't had one in a while. She leaped, killing her prey quickly. With her stomach full and her energy back up, she couldn't help but wonder what had caused the fox from the night before to stop chasing her.

She decided to go back to the scene in broad daylight. She knew that animals like that didn't like the daytime, and she could look for clues as to why it had been so savage, as well as where it was now. She crept back to the site, recognizing the dense bush she had been behind before the attack. She detected the remains of the squirrel the fox had been eating. Disgusted by the way it had left the meal only half eaten and lying on the ground to rot, she covered it in dead leaves before continuing her scan of the region.

Shade could easily identify where the chase had begun by the number of broken twigs, scuffed ground, and absence of leaves in some places where the wind from the fox's approach had blown them away. She followed the trail to the point where it had given up on chasing her. There was a section of fern that was flattened down. Digging in her memory for thoughts from the terrifying event the night before, she remembered that she had heard a thud as if the fox had fallen. Looking back at the site, it looked like this was where it had happened.

She sniffed around the sweep of crushed undergrowth and detected something. It was a sour, sickly sweet and choking scent, like that of death, but stronger, and smelling less like rotting flesh. She wrinkled her nose to drive it out. All at once, she remembered smelling something like it at home. It wasn't the exact scent, but similar. It was when Thunder had gotten sick with a cold. He had lain in bed moaning for days, looking weak and tired. It had taken at least a week for him to get better, and he smelled horrible. Shade shuddered to think that it might be sickness that had felled her pursuer, even if it had managed to drag itself away.

Turning back to her investigation, she detected another smell deep beneath the stench of illness. The smell of people. She recognized it from all the time she'd spent around her owners and their belongings. Intrigued, she focused her hardest on the scent, and identified it right where the fox had been laying. Looking closer, she saw tracks in the few bare patches of earth, leading away into the forest. Or were they leading to the site? The excitement of a mystery filled her, along with a kind of foreboding that the same thing that happened to the fox could happen to her.

For the first time in her life, she felt a little bit scared of the humans that had been there. She walked a little way to where the footsteps of the people began. Just then, she felt a harsh jab in her paw. Looking down, she saw a small, clear, cylinder-shaped object with a fluffy, bright pink pompom on the ground. It had a sharp needle on one end, and it was half filled with a liquid that looked like water. She lifted her paw off of the ground to see blood welling on the spot. A wave of sleepiness abruptly washed over her, and she staggered on the spot. Eyelids slowly closing, she sank to the ground.

As Shade woke up, the sun was already setting. Confused, she tried to remember what had happened before she fell asleep. She remembered going to investigate the fox incident and finding the scent of people all over the area, but after that, her memory was foggy. She shook her head to clear it and looked around. She was still in the spot where the fox had fallen. She shuddered to think that if she hadn't woken up then, the people could have come back to take her away, just like the fox.

Just then, her memory came back to her. She looked down at the small cylinder lying on the ground and bent to sniff it. It smelled strongly of people and had a scent a bit like vinegar, which she had smelled before in her owner's house. Carefully avoiding the needle, she pawed at it. It was empty of the clear liquid that had been in it before. She lifted her scratched paw. There was a thin layer of dried blood, but the pain had gone. Determined not to let the slightly disturbing event deter her from her daily life, she decided to let go of finding out what had happened to the fox.

Shade began to walk around, searching for her next meal. She caught a young rabbit and ate. She returned back to the old tree a couple yards from her den and climbed up, deciding on an early bedtime after the day's events. She drifted off to sleep, her stomach full and feeling content with herself.

As soon as Shade opened her eyes, the cold was the immediate thing on her mind. Crouching huddled in the tree, she hung on tightly to the branch. Without the thick underbrush on the forest floor to protect her from the biting gales, she was exposed to the wind and freezing air. She was shivering all over, and her teeth chattered. Shaky and stiff from the chill, she leaped down from the tree. There was frost on the ground, and her paws burned from it. Even though Shade had begun to grow her winter coat, and her black pelt soaked up heat, she was getting chills. She forgot her hunger in the numbing environment, but exercise would warm her up.

83

She took a brisk stroll through the early morning light to get her blood flowing. She knew that it would be pointless to look for prey when it was still this icy out, so she picked up the pace to a steady jog, trotting around the edge of her territory and pausing occasionally to mark her scent. She stopped at the stream and gazed into the frigid water. She gingerly lapped it up, careful not to get a brain freeze, before moving on.

By then she was fairly warm, and she had gained more energy, even though the sun was barely up. She finished the loop around her territory and headed back to the thicket. All of the trees except for the evergreens were now almost completely stripped of leaves, but the ground was covered in them. She realized that she was going to have to find a warmer place to sleep, or she could freeze. She decided to start looking as soon as possible, which was, in fact, right then. She made a wide sweep of the thicket, meandering her way in a zig-zag pattern through the brush. Finding nothing, she headed in the direction of the creek. She hoped to find something new, as she hadn't explored very much in that area.

It took her several hours to find a likely spot. It was a lean-to made out of a fallen tree, with a wall of thick and tangled branches on one side, and the roots and more branches blocking the other. Shade crept inside, but it was muddy and filled with leaves. It was too

big and open for her anyways, and predators
like foxes could easily get in. She passed it,
and, resignedly, turned to head back to her tree.
She dreaded the thought of spending another
freezing night in the leafless branches of the
tree. She wished that the shelter she had found
had been more secure, but she just didn't feel
safe in it. Leaping back into the boughs of the
tree, she fell asleep, the frigid weather already
setting in.

Shade's morning walk led her back to the
stream. She was surprised at how cold the
water was when she drank. Already the edge of
it had begun to freeze over, though it wasn't
strong enough to support her weight. Today she
had decided on searching for somewhere to

sleep. After her drink, she headed back to the fallen tree that she had considered the day before. Once more she crept inside, but it was no better than earlier. Wondering what else she could do about it, she walked out of the shelter. She sighed. It was no use. Her best bet was to try and repair the other den. *But what if the foxes came back,* she thought. *What would I do then?* She shook her head and wandered back to the stream.

The only place she hadn't explored was across it and close to the road. She knew there would be no chance of finding a good place to stay by the road. She gazed across the fast-flowing water and thought about how to get there. By then the water would be freezing cold, and she didn't know how to swim even if it wasn't. Thinking again, she told herself that she could at least try. She had learned how to climb after all… But it would have to be a different day. She hadn't eaten breakfast yet, and it would take some time to find even the puniest of prey.

She set off along the stream. She'd once seen a water vole there, and she hoped that it might have its nest nearby. Using her nose more than anything else, she discovered a trail of small footprints in the frozen mud. She followed them a short way before they led into the water. Disappointed, she turned around and went back the way she had been going. Just then, she heard a rustling sound in the reeds behind her. She turned and spotted a dark brown pelt disguised in the underbrush. Water vole! Her black fur must have blended in with the dark water just enough for it not to notice her. Excited and relieved about the opportunity that had been presented to her, she tried to pinpoint its location in the weeds. She crept forward. It wasn't difficult to stay silent on the cold earth, and she caught the animal in a matter of seconds. She was grateful for the easy meal. Finishing it down, she looked around aimlessly for something to do.

Shade dipped a paw in the stream. It was cold enough that her paw was already beginning to get numb. She quickly pulled out her paw and flicked the water off of it. She shivered. There was no way she could make herself get in there! As she turned to complete the loop of her domain, the thought of the dangerous temperature still lingered in her mind, but she would have to think about it another time. She had to finish patrolling her territory before she could even begin to think about finding a new one.

Chapter Five

Cold

Shade glanced at the small tool shed as she passed the cabin on her walk around her territory. She had considered this as a possible shelter many times, but it didn't feel right to live so close to the place she had run away from. She wasn't a house cat anymore!

Frustrated, she continued her rounds. She wished there was an easy solution to finding a warmer place to stay. *Other than crossing the stream*, she exasperatedly told herself. She made her way over to the creek and looked across once more.

"How could I get across?" she wondered aloud. It was more than four feet wide, and impossible to jump. She decided that she would at least look in the woods one more time before she even bothered trying to figure out how to cross. Turning to head into the woods, she resolved to finish her patrol later. She walked straight ahead, with the thicket on her right and the cabin on her left. She struggled through a particularly large and thick patch of undergrowth before emerging into a small clearing. The side she had come out of was covered in the same dense underbrush that had kept her from coming in. The other half had pine trees, maple trees, and oaks all spread out, with a few holly bushes in the distance.

She suddenly realized where she was. There were laurels beside her, and a small area of regrowing grass stood out in the center. This was where she had buried Lilac. A wave of sadness washed over her as she slowly walked over to the grave. Soon the grass would regrow and there would be no way of knowing where she laid. She needed a way to mark the place where her mother rested.

She looked around. How would she remember where the grave was? Suddenly, something shimmered out of the corner of her eye. She turned around. As she did, she caught sight of something glinting in the sunlight. She walked in the direction of the light until she came to the roots of an enormous conifer. Ferns and tall grass were clumped around the base, but she pawed it out of the way, revealing a hunk of beautiful crystal, clear as day with sparkling flecks of silver dotted here and there within its depths. It was shaped like one of the fake crystals that had sat on a bookshelf in the cabin, but real. It was half buried in the ground, but enough of it protruded that it was able to catch the sun's rays and shine as if it was a star.

Shade was amazed. It was the perfect memorial to remember the exact place where Lilac lay. She tried to dig around it, but the ground was frozen. She tore one of her claws on the hard earth, and blood began to gather. She licked it away and looked at the crystal. Once more she attempted to get it out of the earth, tugging and levering it bit by bit. After a long time, she managed to pry it up from the earth. She gently gripped the largest column of crystal in her teeth and carried it to Lilac's burial site. Laying it on the center, she walked over to one of the holly bushes and nipped a small twig off. She placed it in front of the stone. She stepped back. It felt good to know that she could now always find where her mother was, even if the grass did regrow. She backed out of the clearing to continue her search, her heart heavy.

As she moved on from the clearing, she

noticed an unusual smell. It smelled like fall time and moth balls. Her curiosity aroused, she attempted to track it. It led away towards where she had been staying. She wondered if it was a different type of prey, like a squirrel or something. As she continued onwards, the smell grew stronger. The bushes ahead rustled as something moved behind them. Something about her size. Something that was definitely not prey.

She stood stock still as it emerged. It was roughly the same size as Lilac had been and had small, beady black eyes. It had a short, flat snout covered in fuzz, and its belly and legs had a coarse looking, dark brown fur. But the thing that scared her the most was its back. It had giant needles poking out in every direction, sharp, striped quills that dragged on the ground as it ambled towards her. She didn't dare to move. It paused and looked at her. She tried hard not to breathe. It moved on. *It must have poor eyesight*, she thought. Her eyes followed it until it disappeared into the bushes on her right. She breathed a sigh of relief and decided that no matter how slow and clumsy it seemed, she would never mess with an animal like that.

Shade watched from her perch in the tree as the sun sank slowly from the sky. The cold weather lingered ominously for a moment before descending down to earth. The air was piercing, and the wind frigid. She was exhausted, but the bitter chill in the air kept her wide awake and shivering. Finally, she made a decision. She scrambled down the tree trunk, her limbs already numb, and walked over to her wrecked den. She glanced around, the memory of waking up to the smell of danger returning. She twitched her ears. *I'm being paranoid*, she thought.

She turned her attention back to her den. Part of the wall was still up, and she curled up inside, pressing her back to the wall. It was hardly any better, but it sheltered her from the worst of the wind, which was horrible in her tree. At last, she fell asleep, her ears, paws, and tail completely numb.

There was a thick layer of frost on the ground. It crunched under Shade's feet as she walked, trembling, from her den. Her breath came in frosty clouds, evaporating up into the bare trees. Her stomach rumbled with a familiar feeling, but no prey would be out when it was this cold. She attempted to open her eyes, but they were glued shut with frozen tears. She began to panic. She rubbed them harshly with her paw until she could see, but her vision was blurry, and her eyes stung. Her nose was encrusted in a coating of hard mucus. She scraped it off with her claws. When she shook it off, she noticed blood. She'd scratched herself. But she couldn't feel it. Her mind seemed to be numb as well. She stumbled a few steps forwards before she paused. She needed to warm up somehow. She began to walk again. She had gone several yards before she picked up the pace to a fast walk, then a slow trot. She jogged the route of her territory, gradually warming up.

She was still a little chilly, but not extremely cold. After a few minutes, she slowed to a walk. She had ended up by the cabin, facing the stream. Her mind had wandered while running. Now she came back to earth. She *hated* the cold, she thought angrily. *I can't stand this much longer.* She had to find a warmer place to sleep. She couldn't stand the feeling of waking up to being so numb that she couldn't even control her own limbs.

She thought of the stream. Did she *have* to

cross it, to find a new den? To her left was where she thought the foxes had come from, behind her the road, and she had never explored to her right. She didn't want to settle that far from her old house. In a small part of her mind, that was still her true home. And, ahead of her, was the stream. She'd answered her own question. But how? There was no way she would even try to swim across. Suddenly, a thought surfaced inside of her. She could make a bridge. Or at least try to.

Filled with a new vigor, she sprinted to the stream. She skidded to a halt, kicking up sand, her paws squelching in the mud. As she steadied her breathing, she tried to judge the distance. It was about four feet wide. She looked around her for something that she could use to start. A long and sturdy stick would work, as long as she could lift it. She scoured the stretch of land. Finding nothing, she tried thinking of other possibilities. She could simply toss small and medium sticks into the stream until it blocked the flow of water, but the problem with that was that the powerful current would simply wash away all of the twigs before she had gathered enough to rise above the water. She shook her head in annoyance. Was anything simple anymore?

She decided that the best thing to do at the moment was to just wander along the stream and look for something, anything, that would help her across. She went in the opposite direction of the cabin and the fox's den, keeping close to the stream's edge. When she reached the edge of her territory, she hesitated. Did she dare to go beyond it? She didn't like the thought of getting lost outside of her known territory and out of reach of any comfort from her past life like the cabin. *Only a few paces*, she convinced herself. It couldn't hurt *that* much if it meant finding a way to survive the frost.

Shade made her way back to her den, tired and defeated. She had traveled further from her territory than she had intended, and it had worn her out walking all the way back. What's more, by the time she'd entered her own land, the sun was down, and prey was scarce. She would have to go to sleep on an empty stomach once more. She curled up in her den. She still hadn't had the time or energy to fully repair it, and the wall sagged inward. She tucked her tail over her nose, the best posture to conserve heat, and drifted off to sleep.

Chapter Six

Scent

Shade sped through the forest, quickly approaching a foolish rabbit that had left its burrow early. She sprinted at full speed, working off the stiffness of cold from her limbs. Taking a daring leap for its hind legs, she caught up to it. She stretched out her claws to their full extent and snared it in its hind fur. Still running, she dragged it backwards until she could get her teeth on its neck. She slowed.

The rabbit was clamped firmly in her jaws, but it was struggling. She pinned it down with her paw and put it out of its misery. She looked around. The chase had taken her to the edge of her territory opposite the cabin. Shade wasn't in this area often, except for when she had been looking for a possible bridge, and she frequently forgot to mark it with her scent. She crouched on the ground to take a bite of her prey, but paused. Something didn't feel right here.

She got up and lifted her nose in the air, taking a whiff of the light breeze that was blowing. An unfamiliar scent wafted to her nostrils. Her whole body tensed up, and her claws flexed in and out, digging into the loam beneath her feet. The wind had stopped entirely. She followed the scent trail determinedly, though it was obscured in some places. It finally led to the edge of her territory, ending at a bush with broken branches and crushed leaves. Shade began to feel her nerves perk up, but not from fear. For the first time in her life, her wildcat ancestors stirred deep inside her. Anger began to build, and her stomach twisted in a knot of rage. It was the scent of another cat. She struggled to keep her cool.

The first, and sensible, thing she should do was to investigate. She stalked up close to the tree that was marked and delicately sniffed it, attempting to keep all of her focus on the task in front of her. Just by scent, she could tell it was a tom, like her brother, and that he was her age. She couldn't get any more information from scent alone, but that was all she needed to know. Outrage pulsed in her veins as she angrily sprayed a challenge on the tree next to the bush. She could sense that that wasn't enough though, so she reared up on her hind legs, tearing at the bark of the tree with thorn sharp claws. She hoped that one day she would sink them into his flesh.

Gradually, Shade calmed. She still couldn't believe that another cat had dared to trespass on her territory, though. That cat was foolish. *Curse him*, she thought furiously. *He'd better stay out of my way. And if he knows what's good for him, he will!* Shade savagely told herself. She sighed. It was no use thinking about what she would do to him if he came back, especially when he wasn't even there. She got back to her rabbit. By then it was cold, but she didn't care. She tore at its flesh, envisioning it being the ignorant cat that had just challenged her. Her anger melted away, giving way to a feeling of exhaustion. It was still only late morning, but Shade was ready for a nap. She hadn't been tired enough to take one in a while, and it was hard to fall asleep against the bright light, but she eventually dropped off. The sun felt good, soaking into her black fur and warming her to the core. Her dreams were pleasant, and her sleep deep.

Shade stretched. She'd only slept for a half hour, but it had refreshed her and given her new vigor. She had forgotten to do her regular patrol that morning, and now she began the loop. She walked straight ahead, towards the road, until she got to where she usually marked her scent. She walked along the border a few paces before stopping to spray on a dead bush. She meandered her way towards the cabin, pausing here and there to mark her territory. The anger from earlier had gone completely, and now all she felt was a kind of duty to keep others out.

She strolled confidently across her old people's gravel driveway and marked her scent on the little tool shed. She flexed her foreclaws, enjoying this pleasantly warm day. It hadn't been this warm since the first frost. And even though she could still see her breath coming out of her in thick white clouds, she wasn't quite as cold as she would have been if the day was as cold as it had been lately. She trotted away from the plot and towards the stream, her spirits high.

She arrived in a matter of minutes and immediately lapped at the water, eagerly gulping it down. Feeling refreshed and energetic, she continued on her way. She jogged along the edge of the water, gazing longingly across. The trees on that side were spaced rather widely apart by the stream, but she could tell that they grew thicker further on.

Most of them looked like some type of fir, but there were a few skinny maples scattered here and there. In the middle of it all there was a boulder like the one she slept under now, sticking up out of the ground in the middle. It looked ancient, with lichen and moss growing all over and covering the true color of the rock. The whole scene was beautiful. As Shade came back to earth, she realized she'd stopped walking altogether. A bit frustrated with herself but glad she'd taken a moment to look it over, she started walking again.

Once more her nerves tensed up as she rounded a corner and broke away from the stream. She was nearing the place where she had first scented the stranger. She wanted to try and keep her anger at bay, and she took deep breaths as she came close to the tree. She paused every few seconds to mark her scent. After what felt like ages, she came to the marker. She could just make out her own claw marks, but both her and the tom's scent marks had faded in the past few hours. She sprayed a warning on the tree, half hoping that he would not heed, just so that she could talk some sense into him. She sighed deeply. Again, there was no point in getting worked up and wasting her energy on someone who wasn't there. She finished that particular side of her territory, marking it every so often, before she broke off and headed deeper into the woods to search for her next meal.

Shade somehow managed to sleep through the night, but she shivered like mad the whole time. After that blessedly warm day, it just got colder. And colder. And colder.

Shade woke with a start. It hadn't gotten any warmer, even though the sun was already beginning to rise. She shook out her fur, fluffing it out in an attempt to warm up, even just a little bit. Reluctantly, she rose to her feet, stretching and yawning. Her limbs were shaking and her teeth chattering, but she resiliently tried to stop them. She decided to get an early start on her patrol to warm up, and besides, she wasn't hungry yet. She could catch prey during the loop of her territory. She set off, heading in the direction of the road. She always started here, and it was simply routine by then. She walked briskly along the edge of her territory, spraying her scent occasionally.

As she left the street, its roar became distant. She neared the cabin after what felt like a long walk. She had just recently realized how small she had been when they first escaped the cabin, which explained why it had taken them so long to get to the road. She had never felt the need to scent mark the area around the cabin, as the people living there scared off most other animals. But, this time, she did, just to be safe. The invading cat could loop around her territory, scent masked by the road, and end up here. By the time she had gotten to the stream, her hunger had started to kick in. She sniffed the air in hopes that she might catch the scent of an animal like a water vole.

Luck must have been on her side that day, because out of nowhere she saw a flash of gray brown fur right in front of her. She crouched instinctively, hiding her dark fur in the dried reeds. She peered through the thick stalks of the plants. She could spot her prey rustling the weeds on the bank. The small water mammal must not have seen her. As quietly as she could, she crept forward. When she was only a few paces behind it, she pounced. Her front paws landed on its tail, pinning it down. It squealed and tried to run, but she grasped it in her jaws and killed it quickly. She ate slowly, thanking her good fortune. Her belly full, she continued walking along the stream. She never marked her territory by the stream for fear of scaring away all of the animals that lived there, so she only paused for a drink. The water was ice cold and made her teeth ache, but she was thirsty.

As she walked farther along, she came to the side of territory where that *other* cat had marked his scent. Once again, something didn't feel right. Wasting no time marking this part, she bounded forward. His scent was here. And fresh. It led deep into the woods of her territory. *Her* territory! *He'd better get out!* she thought furiously.

Not bothering to stalk him, she raced

forwards, hard on his trail. In the distance she could pick out a flash of brown and black pelt. As she crashed through the undergrowth, she began to smell fear. This cat knew she was here. She could hear him as he started running towards the thicket, but she pulled ahead of him. Heart racing, she dashed in front of the long-haired tabby, blocking his path. He skidded to a halt, eyes wide. A growl rumbled deep in her throat, and her eyes flashed. She hissed a warning. But the amber eyed tom just stared at her. He smelled strongly of fear, but she could almost detect a hint of admiration. No! She didn't want that.

"What do you want?" she spat fiercely. She glared at him. He still seemed to show a little bit of respect, almost confidence. Angered even more, she advanced dangerously on him. At last, she could pick out a tiny bit of submission.

"I-I-I don't know! I-I just- I wanted to meet you... I-I guess..." he stuttered. He looked genuinely scared now.

"Well, the only version of me you'll ever get to meet is the angry one, cause I'm about to rip your ugly face right off!" she growled.

"But-"

She cut him off. "Get. Out. Of. My. Territory. Now! Before I make you!" she howled.

"But-"

Was this cat really too stupid to understand a threat like that? She launched herself at him, raking her claws across his ears, blood spraying the ground. He yelped and feebly tried to defend himself. He landed a scratch on her nose, and she could feel blood welling on the spot, but this only made her angrier.

Screeching, she lunged. He turned to run, but she caught his back leg, tripping him and biting down on it. He lashed out, tearing her ear, but he was scared more than anything else, and she could sense it. She sank her teeth deeper, but let go almost immediately. She didn't want to seriously injure this idiot, but no intruder like him would get out of her territory unharmed.

She stopped to let him get up, but only for a moment. He scrambled out of her way as

Shade snarled fiercely at him. She chased him to the edge of her border, and gave him a last, satisfying scratch on the haunches before allowing him to run away into the woods on the other side. As the crash of underbrush faded, Shade turned around. The fight, though short, had both exhausted and exhilarated her, and she was ready for a rest.

As Shade crouched in her den, she ran over the day's events in her head. She licked gingerly at the scratches the tom had given her. It was nothing serious. She thought about the wounds she had inflicted. *He had been ignorant*, the small part of her that was still angry thought. But even though he had deserved it, she wondered if she'd been too

harsh. Maybe he was just a little…
inexperienced.

Chapter Seven

Water

That night, the wind howled. Small particles of sharp ice pelted down in sheets from the dark sky. The sun had set only a half hour ago, but the world was black as midnight, a thick, gray and black carpet of cloud covering the sky. Distantly, thunder rumbled, and Shade shivered. The icy wind was strong enough to knock her off her paws if she dared to leave her small shelter. She closed her eyes. This storm was worse than any she'd ever experienced in her life.

She crouched, shaking and trembling furiously. Even though she was awake, she could feel her nose running and freezing up. Shade coughed and wiped her nose on the back of a paw. She took a deep breath, trying to steady her breathing. Her limbs were beginning to stiffen from the cold, and she sneezed. She sniffed and blinked her eyes rapidly. They had started watering, and some of the tears turned to ice immediately. She didn't want to close her eyes, though, for fear of them being glued shut. Her whole body ached with the cold, and she couldn't stop her teeth from chattering. Her ears were numb by then, but somehow, she eventually managed to fall asleep.

Shade woke up in the middle of the night. The storm was still raging outside. She was shivering, but her head felt hot. Her nose was running non-stop, and she sneezed abruptly. She felt woozy, and her eyes watered some more. *I hate this feeling!* she thought. She shook her head to try and clear some of her head ache, but it just made her feel dizzy. She tried falling asleep, but it was difficult, and she spent most of the night drifting off then waking up again. Fevered dreams intruded her sleep and left her sitting wide eyed and shaking on the floor of her den.

Shade arose to a white blanket of snow covering the ground. It glistened and shone brightly in the early morning light, muffling all sounds. While she was asleep, the fierce storm had settled into steady snowfall. She blinked to open her eyes. Her paws and ears were still numb from the cold, and she shivered. The runny nose and cough were gone from the night before, and her head felt surprisingly clear. She sat up and peered around the broken wall at the snow. She had never experienced anything like it. The ferns, even though they were all dead, had kept the snow from piling up against her den, and she had a clear pathway outside.

Cautiously, she crept out of her den. As she exited, a crisp, icy smell greeted her nose. She placed a wary paw on the snow. It enveloped her foot, coming all the way up to her foreleg before she felt solid ground beneath her paw. Relieved that it didn't go on forever, she put her other paw in. The snow crunched satisfyingly beneath her. She enjoyed the sound but was too excited about exploring this new white world to waste time.

No longer careful, she bounded forward, spraying snow all over the place and staining her black fur with spatters of white powder. She dashed around, scooping snow off the ground and flinging it into the air to watch it float back down to earth. Shade played like a little kitten for several minutes straight, but even though she was excited, she knew she had to calm down. There was no point in going hungry while she was busy playing around. With a happy feeling lingering inside her, Shade decided to try and catch some prey before she went on patrol, for she doubted that the cat would come back after the lesson she'd taught him. It was still frigid out, and Shade could see her breath, so she didn't expect to see many other animals outside that day. It surprised her to see a small gray mouse pop its head unexpectedly out of the snow. Before she could get a good look at it, it dived back underneath. She wondered how to stalk it. She would have to wait for it to come out again before she could even try anything.

She sat there for several minutes until it came out once more. She stood up and took a step forward, but the thin layer of ice that was on top crunched loudly when she walked. She crouched, hoping that the mouse couldn't detect her dark shape in the snow. Her prey didn't notice. *I guess I'll have to try something else.*

Remembering the first time she had hunted for herself, she wondered if she could just leap all the way over to it and reach it before it even knew she was there. It wasn't that far away, so she might as well attempt to do it. She tensed her body up, ready to spring. All at once, she leaped as far as she could, almost reaching the mouse, but not quite. Startled, it stopped sniffing the air and ran across the top of the snow, leaving tiny prints. Shade dashed after it, dodging trees and bushes and kicking up snow. It scurried a couple of feet before disappearing under the blanket of white.

But Shade didn't give up on it. She reached her paw down the tunnel it left and pulled it out by its tail, squealing. She pinned it down and finished it off. She ate, then got to her paws and started her patrol. She reached the road and continued towards the cabin. She had almost forgotten about the storm before the snow, but here she could see a bit of damage. A thin tree had been knocked over, and a bush was stripped of all the dead leaves that had been hanging on. A little shaken, she moved on to the stream, occasionally spraying her mark and enjoying the interesting and refreshing scent of snow. As she walked along the edge of the stream, she noticed that a thin layer of ice was forming on the edge. She walked up to the edge of the freezing water and carefully rested a paw on it. Still keeping three of her legs on safe ground, she put some weight onto her paw. The ice creaked and groaned, and she hurriedly picked it up. Then an idea occurred to her. *If the ice got strong enough, would it be strong enough that I would be able to cross on it?*

The thought lingered in her mind as she walked along the stream. She came to the middle of it and paused. Up ahead, she could see something laying across the water. It looked like it was about four inches wide. She ran towards it. She neared it in a matter of seconds, skidding to a halt on the cold sand. She peered out over the water. A thin tree was stretched across it, its roots on the opposite bank and its few branches now blocking the way in front of her.

It must have been knocked down by the wind in the storm, she thought excitedly. *This could be my way across!* She weaved her way in between the spindly branches until she reached the edge of the water. She placed her front paws on the trunk, praying that it would support her weight. It bent and wobbled a little bit, but other than that, she was fine. *I might as well go now,* she thought. At last, she could explore a new territory, find a warmer, safer den, and escape the fear of the fox ever coming back. Relieved, she stepped all the way onto the tree and began to cross. Slowly and carefully, she placed one paw in front of the other. She was about halfway when suddenly the thin tree started to sag towards the water. Her weight must have been a bit too much for the little sapling. The middle part was underwater, but it was just thick enough to keep her paws dry. She held her breath. The tree swayed in the current, and Shade struggled to keep her balance. Did she risk dashing across, or could she make it by going slowly?

Shade made up her mind. Not wanting to risk the tree sagging farther, she took a deep breath and dashed across. She was almost there when her foot hit a knob on the trunk. Pain shot up her leg, and she yelped. Losing her footing, her back legs fell into the water. She panicked. Scrabbling at the smooth bark with her claws, she tried heaving herself back onto the log. The current dragged at her fur, threatening to sweep her away. She kicked at the water, treading her back legs, and trying to push herself back on. The cold was piercing. She bit back a yowl.

Just then, she felt something brush against her leg. She thrashed in the water, and, in her panic, she let go of the log. She screeched, pumping her legs as hard and fast as they would go and struggling against the current. Her head dunked underwater, and for a stunning moment, she thought it was over. But then her head broke the surface. She gasped and choked on the water, coughing. She took a deep breath, and a new determination filled her.

A thick mass of roots stuck out of the side of the bank. She kicked out strongly and moved towards the clump. As the current swept her further away from the tree, she could see the roots approaching. She rushed towards them, still struggling to keep her head above the water. She was barely a foot away from them when an extremely strong wave of water swept her under. Shade panicked, and tried to swim back, but the stream's iron grip dragged her deeper still. Water filled her nose, eyes, and mouth, and her vision blurred. Bubbles escaped from her nose, and it felt as if a giant hand was squeezing her lungs. She strained to reach the surface, and finally her paw cleared it. She pumped her legs and paddled as hard as she could, and at last, her head broke the surface. She gasped, sucking in air. Breathing had never felt so good.

She looked around her, searching for the roots. Surprisingly, they were still in view, and she paddled over to them as fast as she could, straining against the flow of water. She thought about just trying to get out of the water where she was, but the bank was steep and crumbly, and probably wouldn't support her weight. The lump of roots could be her only chance.

Suddenly, another wave washed over her muzzle. A rush of panic seized her at the thought of going under again, and it spurred her on until she reached the tangle of roots. She stretched out a paw and gripped the cluster of vine-like roots. Paw over paw and hardly daring to look back, she climbed precariously out of reach of the water lapping at her back paws. Soaking wet, Shade hauled herself onto dry land.

Panting hard and freezing cold, her panic and fear was replaced by a powerful exhaustion. She sat hunched over, trying to steady her breathing. Her sides heaved, and she started coughing again. She hacked up a mouthful of water, spilling it at her paws. She choked and coughed, panting until her breathing was back to normal. Shade took a deep breath. Just then, she heard a splash. In the distance, she could make out the tree she'd used to try to cross as it fell into the water. *That was close*, she thought. *A little* too *close*.

Abruptly, she realized that her way back was gone. She looked back across the water. Now she had no way of going back. Five months had passed since she had escaped the house with Lilac and her siblings, but it still felt like home. She realized that she was going to miss the thicket and going to visit her old home.

Almost fully recovered, Shade wandered around this new part of the woods. It was odd, having no idea about where she was going. All she knew was that the deeper into the forest she went, she was more likely to find a new and warmer den. She walked slowly, taking in the scenery and making mental notes of everything.

Suddenly, a cough tore through her throat, interrupting her peaceful walk. She coughed again. She couldn't stop. She wheezed and gasped for air. Eventually, it subsided, but her throat felt raw. She sat down, panting. The feeling that she'd felt on the night of the storm had returned. She felt sick. Was she coming down with something, like Thunder had before they'd escaped? If so, the cold would only make it worse. She had to find a den, and soon. Shade wandered among the trees, searching for something that would make a safe den. The sun hung low in the sky, glowing softly and shedding its blood red light over the ground. Shade sighed. *I'm going to need luck on my side if I'm going to find a den before dark*, she thought hopelessly. As she continued on her way, she thought about her old den. She wondered if she would be able to find anything like it in her new territory. She picked up the pace, racing the setting sun.

Just as the sun slipped out of the sky, Shade sighted something. It was a wall of rock, towering hundreds of feet above her. She gazed up at it, awed. The cliff face was jagged and filled with cracks and crags and rocks that stuck out sideways at odd angles. Silhouetted against the last of the dying light, it looked like a huge beast. To her left, there ran a gigantic gash from the top of the cliff, all the way to the bottom. It was several feet deep and filled with even more ledges. It looked as if an enormous cat had run its claws all the way down, leaving an open wound in the rocks.

Shade walked slowly towards the formation, her eyes roving around the area. At last, something caught her eye. It was a huge boulder, more than five times her size. It looked like it had broken loose from the cliff and fallen, rolling until it stopped where it was, a few yards away from the edge of the slope. *Perfect,* she thought. It reminded her of her old den in her first territory. Though she wouldn't have time to turn it into a proper den that night, she could make a temporary shelter in the cracks between some of the rocks above. She walked over to the wall and slid her way into a deep crag low to the ground, with a few dead leaves on the inside. She curled up inside and fell asleep almost immediately.

Chapter Eight

Claw

For the second time that year, snow covered the ground. The morning light was magnified by the pure white layer, and it shone brightly into Shade's makeshift den as she stretched. She climbed from the cliff's side, landing with a soft crunch on the ground. She raised her head to the sky and took a whiff of the cool, crisp scent of fresh air. The snow muffled everything, and her breath came out in wispy clouds of vapor, rising in the air until they evaporated. She walked slowly towards the forest, her paws already beginning to numb. As she entered the vast spread of trees, her stomach rumbled. Taking heed, she started to sniff the air in search of a scent trail that an early rising prey animal could have left.

She made her way around a thick tree and caught the scent. It was that of a rabbit, and wasn't too far away. She could reach it in a matter of minutes, but she would have to be careful of the crisp and icy snow. She stalked quietly through the trees and underbrush, the scent getting stronger every second. Finally, she reached a particularly prickly bush. Behind it, she could make out the small form of a rabbit moving about in the snow. She crouched low, hoping that the spindly branches were dense enough to conceal her. Slowly, she crept along the edge of the bush. When she got to the side, she planned her next move carefully. If she was quick enough, she could burst from her side of the bush, corner the rabbit against its thorns, and capture it.

Thinking that it was the best option, she quickly pushed off of her hind legs, veering round the corner of the bush. The rabbit sprang away from her, sprinting into the woods to her left. Wasting no time in being disappointed, she dashed after it, her paws crunching loudly as she ran after her prey. Gradually, she began to catch up. She sped alongside the rabbit,

ready to reach out and snatch it into her jaws.
She stretched her neck as far as it would go,
and grasped the struggling creature in her
mouth. She skidded to a halt, the now dead
rabbit hanging in her jaws. She laid it on the
ground, a small amount of blood seeping from
the wound in its neck. She ate slowly, looking
around her in amazement. The chase had taken
her to the edge of her territory. It looked so
much different now that the snow blanketed the
ground. The trees were now completely
stripped of leaves, and the white dusting
covered some of the thicker branches.

As she finished her meal, she stood up. All
of her senses were hyper. Something wasn't
right with the way the woods had suddenly

grown quiet. Just like the night when she'd seen the fox. She quickly dug a hole in the ground and stuffed the remains of the rabbit inside. She didn't want the fox to detect the scent of blood and come to her. Slowly and as silently as she could, Shade crept into the forest. On a day as cold as this, there was no chance that she would get herself stuck in a tree for the night. She had to get back to the temporary den. It was the safest and warmest place possible for her to shelter in. She made her way through the trees, her fur standing on end. At last, she neared her makeshift den. She could just make out the side of the cliff through the bare trees. Relief flooded her, but she didn't dare to go any faster.

Just then, the dreaded sound of growling could be heard. And it was coming from her den. Shade stood stock still, frozen in fear. She watched in horror as the huge creature emerged from behind a boulder. Its eyes roved around the landscape, searching for her. Shade kept her eyes glued to the fox as she began backing away. She instantly regretted it. Its head turned, its eyes quickly focusing on her. *If this is what it's like to be hunted,* she thought, *I'll never stalk prey again.* The growls increased, and suddenly the fox sprang forward, bounding towards her. She turned tail and ran, adrenaline rushing, heart pumping, lungs burning with both heat and cold. She could hear the fox crashing through the bushes behind her, and made herself go faster. Her muscles burned from running, but she kept going. She could feel its breath on her hind quarters. She closed her eyes and ran faster than she ever had in her life.

As she opened her eyes, the sight of what was surely death greeted her – the stream. She put on a burst of speed, hoping that she could get far enough away from her hunter that she could then swerve to avoid the churning water. She reached the edge of the water and turned to run. But the fox was right in front of her, already leaping for her throat. She dodged to one side, and it skidded on the sandy bank, almost falling in. She shook off the feeling of shock and decided that if she was ever going to live peacefully, she would have to kill it. She lunged onto its back, latching on and dragging her claws through its matted fur. With a howl of rage, it flung her off.

She landed with a thud on the snowy forest floor. Snow filled her eyes, but she could sense that the fox was near. She rolled away just as it leapt. Standing up, she flicked the snow out of her eyes and turned to face her enemy. It made the first move, its vicious teeth clamping onto her shoulder. She screeched in pain and lashed out with her claws, catching it on the nose. Blood seeped through her fur as she tried once more to get it to let go. She thrashed and flailed, her tail whipping it in the face, but each movement only made its grip tighten on her.

The pain was overwhelming, and she squeezed her eyes closed.

In an instant, the pressure was gone. The fox had let her go. Blood streamed forth from the wound in her shoulder, and she staggered. As she found her footing, she realized that the fox was looking back across the stream at something that was moving in the underbrush. Seizing the opportunity, she rushed at the fox, bowling it over and clamping her jaws on the back of its throat. It snarled and pawed at her back with its hind legs, leaving behind scratch marks and redness. She raked her claws across its face, at the same time letting go of its neck. Her claws slashed one of its eyes, and it yelped, jumping backward. It growled and backed off, circling her until her back was to the stream. Eyes wide with fear, she backed up, stopping only when she could feel the freezing water biting at her ankles.

As the fox got ready to leap, Shade had an idea. It lunged at her, flying through the air, but she was ready. She scrambled out of the way just as it hit the ground. She ran a few paces away from the stream and turned just in time to see the fox splash into the stream and be swept away by the current.

Shade limped all the way to the small cave in which she had slept the night before. The wounds she had been dealt were encrusted in dried blood, and the shoulder that the fox had bitten was swollen. Its teeth had nipped one of her ears, and the tip was torn off completely. It was still bleeding heavily, and pain seemed to come from every single part of her body. She clambered awkwardly up to the hollow in the rocks and squeezed inside. The agony she felt was unbelievable. Just as she was about to sit down, the whole world went black. She'd passed out from the pain.

The sun had slipped behind the mountains in front of her by the time Shade came to. Her shoulder and legs were stiff, and her head throbbed from when she had hit it on the hard floor of her cave. Slowly, she sat up. All of the bleeding had stopped, leaving behind an awful tenderness. She tried moving her shoulder, but a spasm ran through it, stopping her. Her ear was still stinging, but she was glad she hadn't suffered worse. Exhaustion made her eyelids heavy, and she laid down. With her many hurts still throbbing, she fell asleep.

Shade slept through the entire day, letting her scratches and bites heal themselves. When she finally awoke, the pain was almost gone. Except for the ache in her shoulder, she felt relatively good. There was still a thin layer of snow that lingered on the ground, but beneath that she could make out a few little sprouts of green. She sat up and looked out of the small opening in the cliff's side. She purred with pleasure. She'd gotten rid of the fox.

Chapter Nine

Back

The sun rose slowly, and so did Shade. For the first time in a while, she slept without being freezing cold. She slowly opened one eye and yawned. She was still cold, but not as much as she had been. All of her wounds seemed to have healed over the past day, and even her bad shoulder felt better. Happy at her success of the day before and eager to make an even better den, she sat up, careful not to hit her head.

Leaping gracefully out of the shelter, she strode over to the boulder. She began circling it, wondering how she would turn it into a proper den. Maybe she could hollow out the ground beside it, and sleep *under* the boulder, a bit like her old den. Thinking that this was definitely worth a try, she started searching for anything that would help her get started. At last, she found what she was looking for. It was a small hole, probably an abandoned mole hole. It was just wide enough for her to fit both of her front paws inside without getting them stuck, and it faced away from the cliff, so that she could come out of her den in the morning and immediately see what was going on in the woods, a sure advantage.

Excitedly, she began scratching at the hole, making it wider and wider. The earth was frozen in some places, but the boulder had sheltered most of it from frosting too much. She dug away vigorously, and in a couple of minutes, it was as wide as her head, and two inches deep. Suddenly, she realized just how much work it would take. She'd probably spend at least a day before she could even fit inside. But she had to! She went back to work, digging harder and faster than ever, and trying to ignore the ache that was coming back to her shoulder.

It was midday before Shade even considered stopping. Her claws, paws, and all four legs ached from clawing away at the ground, and she realized just then how hungry she was. She hadn't even had dinner the night before. This made up her mind. Leaving her backbreaking task behind, Shade dashed into the forest.

As she neared the stream, the rich scent of her favorite prey made her mouth water. Squirrel. She could see it scuffling around on the ground, trying to locate a long-lost nut that it had buried in the fall. The breeze blew its scent towards her, so it had no way of knowing that she was there, unless it saw her. Carefully, she stalked forward. When she was only a couple of feet away, she pounced. The squirrel dropped its nut and bolted, but the wrong way. It skidded on the sandy beach of the stream and made a sharp left turn to avoid the churning water. Shade had expected the stream coming up, and she veered away before the squirrel to block its path. It ran straight into her claws. She trapped it and her teeth did the rest.

As she finished her squirrel, she thought about the encounter with the fox. Was it really fair that all of the prey animals she hunted had to live in constant fear of a predator killing them? She paused. There was nothing she could do about it. In the end, someone was always going to die. Either she would starve, or her prey would be eaten. Still, she felt a little bit guilty that she hadn't considered how scary life was as someone's prey. With the gap in her stomach filled, she was eager once more to get working and take her mind off the thought.

Shade returned to her den refreshed and full of life. She stretched and flexed her claws before she walked over to the hole she had begun to dig. The dirt had softened since morning, and it was much easier to make progress. By the time the sun was close to setting, she already had a tunnel leading under the boulder that was about two feet long. She backed out of it and shook the dirt off of her pelt. Proud of her work, but still not finished, she crept back in to start hollowing out the area where she would sleep. She scratched vigorously at the ceiling, dirt showering on her. She blinked to keep it out of her eyes. She worked steadily, only pausing occasionally to scrape dirt out of the hollow. Eventually, she stopped to take a break. She'd dug a hole that could fit about three of her, and the ceiling was high enough for her not to hit her head.

Peering out the tunnel, she realized that it was already dark out. She'd lost track of time. She crouched down and squeezed her way out. She was pleased to notice that it was much warmer in her new den. Even so, the bare earth that covered the floor in the shelter was cold and uncomfortable to lay on. But that didn't matter. What mattered was that she had a den that would keep her warm.

She crawled back inside, glad for how much of a difference it made being inside rather than out. She could hear the wind howling, but not a breeze touched her here. She felt content, happy that she had at last found a place that she could settle down in. Within minutes she had drifted off into a deep and peaceful sleep.

The next day, Shade sniffed around the roots of an evergreen tree. *Definitely home to a mouse,* she thought. She could pick out a tiny hole just in between two of the largest roots. She sniffed some more. The mouse wasn't home, she could tell that, so that meant it had to be in the woods somewhere. Her stomach rumbled, but she wasn't quite painfully hungry yet, which was better than when she was almost starving. She'd been needing more and more food to sustain her growing body, and now she usually had at least two mice a meal.

If she got started now, she could track the mouse and find more by mid-morning. The trail led towards the cliff, and she began tracking it. Before long, she could see the small creature shuffling under a pile of leaves, searching for food. She pounced quickly and devoured her meal.

Today, she was going to explore every inch of her territory. Already, she was beginning to get excited to see what else was in store for her in the new woods. Her second mouse forgotten, she took a glance about her. It was difficult to see more than a few yards ahead. The bushes and underbrush blocked her path. Solving this problem with ease, Shade leaped skillfully into the low branches of the nearest tree, an old and thick trunked cedar. She climbed from branch to branch, in no hurry, until she was just over halfway up the tree. She was high enough that she could see the tops of some of the smaller trees.

As she settled on a sturdy branch, the beauty and peace of being in the air came back to her. The smell of the cold wind refreshed her, and the view was amazing from up on her perch. She began to relax, but in an attentive way. She tucked her paws under her and gazed around at the woods spread out below her. It had been such a long time since she'd been in a tree, and she began to relive how peaceful it was.

After a while, Shade stretched. She realized that she'd been daydreaming. She blinked her eyes and looked around. It was high noon, and the sun hung lazily in the sky waiting to be enveloped by a quickly approaching mountain of clouds. She smelled the air. Rain was on its way. She looked towards the precipice and to where her den was. Just then, a flock of large, shiny-feathered black birds took wing from the trees on top of the cliff, cawing. The hair on the back of her neck rose. What had scared them into flight?

Gradually, the clouds rolled in to cover the sun, and darkness fell. Shade shivered. She leapt down from the branch and began her silent descent. She was going to investigate. She crept along the forest floor, quickly but carefully. In moments she had reached her den.

Something had been here. Or someone, rather. The strong smell of rain disguised the scent. Shade scanned the bushes around her before looking up at the cliff. *Should I stay in my den?* she thought. Whatever had scared the birds could be dangerous. No. She had to go. She couldn't have an intruder in her territory when she had just moved in, especially if it was something that would scare away her meals. She'd already dealt with a fox, so there was no point in being scared. Foxes were probably the most dangerous thing the woods had to offer.

With her mind made up, she headed towards the cliff. She had to get whoever it was out, before they came back to her den. With a new sense of urgency, she started off to the right of the cliff face. It seemed to be the fastest way up, and with a storm on the way, it was best to get this over with.

The ground in front of her sloped up, and the trees thinned out as she hurried onward. The sky grew darker with every minute, but she wasn't going to turn back now. She picked up the pace until she was rushing up the hill. The scent of the intruder was getting closer. Nerves pricked her, and she looked around the dim forest anxiously. What if it was a fox? It didn't matter. She'd faced a fox before. She had to keep going.

In the distance, thunder rumbled. Shade ran the last few yards. She'd reached the top of the cliff. From here, the woods seemed to go on forever. She stopped, breathing heavily, and stared across the forest. She could see everything. As if in a trance, she stepped forward, towards the cliff's edge. To her right, far, far away, she could see the clearing where her cabin was. Sadness ached inside of her. Straight ahead, and not too far, she could see the stream. Would she ever go back across? Worry crept into her mind. And, in the distance, she could see the road. The place where she'd lost everything. Her mother. Her siblings. Her life. Grief bubbled to the surface.

Abruptly, thunder clapped, snapping Shade out of her daze. She shook her head and turned her back on the scenery. It was stupid of her to think about these things. It wasn't as if she could go back. She turned her back to the edge of the cliff and scanned the area. There was a clearing at the top of the cliff, but in front of her, the woods sloped down and away. To her right was a mound of white rocks, and a clear path led away towards them. The sky was pitch black now. She sniffed the air. Nothing. She tried again, and there, floating faintly on the breeze, was the scent of a cat. Him. The cat who she'd already fought off. The cat who thought she was weak. The cat who'd intruded once, and now twice!

Her heart pounded, and her blood boiled. No. NO. NO! She would not let this happen again! She was going to make sure that he understood that she meant it. He already got a warning. Now, she was going to have to deal with him the proper way. Her eyes blazed. She crouched low, her fur on end and her ears pinned back. She followed the scent, her tail tense with anger. Around the mound of rocks, she headed down the path. His scent was getting stronger.

The bushes ahead rustled, and Shade stopped. She was done stalking. She rushed forward into the bushes. She collided with the tom, knocking the breath out of him. He yowled as they tumbled out of the bush and onto the path. Shade stood up, pinning him to the ground. Seething, she slashed her claws across his face. Blood welled on the spot, and she saw him wince. She curled her lip in disgust. He was so *soft*!

"You. How dare you. How DARE YOU!"

She scratched him on the muzzle once more. She snarled, and he leapt up. There was fear in his eyes, but that wasn't enough. As he tried to run, she tore after him. She sprang onto his back, sinking her teeth into his scruff. He screeched in pain and threw her off. She landed with a thump on the ground. She jumped to her feet and rushed at him again.

"GET OUT!" she roared.

He backed away, but she was already upon him. She was a whirlwind of piercing claws and needle-sharp teeth. She shredded his ears with her claws and bit down hard on his neck again. He attempted to turn and defend himself, but she was already there, raking her claws across his flank. He howled and finally threw her off. She stood on her hind legs, ready to crush him, but he stood up as well. Thinking fast, she put her front legs out in front of her, her paws pressing on his shoulders. He twisted in her grip, but she wrestled him to the ground.

From then on, they were a screaming knot of fangs and claws. Blood and fur flew everywhere as they rolled around. Every time the cat landed a blow, she would deal an equally brutal one. Her shoulders and legs ached from the hard ground, and her many scratches stung, but she refused to give in.

Just then, the tom slipped away. Out of reach, he started running blindly, the gray clouds turning day into night. Shade sprinted after him. Suddenly, he skidded to a halt and turned, his eyes wide with fear. Shade reared up on her back legs, posed to strike. Thunder clapped and lightning lit up the sky, illuminating the scene.

As Shade came crashing down upon him, a chilling screech of terror filled the air. She'd found out why he'd stopped.

Chapter Ten

Oak

Shade stood at the edge of the cliff, her heart pounding. Fury twisted inside of her. He was there. The stupid, ignorant, arrogant cat that had trespassed and made fun of her, was there, hanging on desperately to the cliff's edge. She felt a jolt of anger. So what if he died, fallen off a cliff because he had dared to seek her out? But she couldn't. She couldn't kill a cat. She stepped forward and looked him in the eye. She saw fear and sadness. No. She could never let him fall. Never. She couldn't let him lose his grip!

Shade leaned towards him and gripped his scruff in her jaws. She heaved his weight clear of the dark, gaping cliff and dropped him on the ground. She straightened up. He slowly rose to his feet, not once taking his eyes off her face. At that moment, the clouds let loose. Rain poured from the sky, soaking Shade and dripping off of her whiskers.

"Thank you," he whispered. Shade looked at him, her heartbeat quickening.

"You're welcome," she replied softly. "Why? Why did you come here?"

"I-I don't know. I just... I... I don't know

what happened to me. I just suddenly felt the…
the urge to look for you. To find you."

For a second, Shade was silent. *He must be
mad*, she thought. But a small part of her felt
the same way. She shook her head.

"You shouldn't have. I might have killed
you." Her throat tightened at the thought. "All I
wanted was to live my life. Alone. To take care
of myself, and-and find my own food and
shelter and-"

He cut her off. "But why? Why do it alone
when you could have help? Company? A…
friend?"

Shade stared. A friend? She hadn't been
around another cat since Lilac had died. That
was over six months ago.

"What's your name?" she asked apprehensively. Why would he want to befriend her? She'd never even met him.

"Oak," he said. He seemed nervous but excited that she had asked. "Who are you?"

"I'm…" Shade paused. *Should I tell him? Should I lie?* "I'm… Shade," she finished. Her ears began to feel hot, and a warm feeling began to grow in her stomach. She looked away.

"Oh." He stared blankly at her, but she could sense his sadness. She hadn't meant to turn away like that. "I guess I should… well… go." He turned to leave, his ears pulled back and his tail dragging sorrowfully in the mud.

"Wait! Come with me," Shade said,

hurrying to catch up with him. She couldn't leave him to go back the way he came, all alone while the rain showered down on him. "I…I thought you might want shelter," she spoke in an undertone.

"Yes. I do want shelter," Oak whispered the words, but they seemed to have a deeper meaning. Affection for the willful tom filled her, and she started to lead him through the trees and towards her den.

Mud spattered Shade's chest fur as she walked to the tunnel of her den. She paused at the entrance, letting Oak go in front of her. The harsh pounding of rain faded as she entered her den behind him. Water streamed off of Shade's shoulders and pooled on the dirt floor of the hollow. She blinked to keep it out of her eyes. A million feelings seemed to swirl inside Shade's head. Confusion, anger, sadness, and worry flew through her. But there was one feeling she couldn't place. It made her feel jittery and warm. It was something she'd only ever felt with her siblings and her mother.

Love. As soon as she recognized it, she hated it. She couldn't fall in love with *him*! She wanted to be free. She didn't want to have to look after someone all the time! All of a sudden, the walls and ceiling of her den seemed to press into her. Her breathing quickened, and she started to back away. Oak turned to face her.

"Are you okay?" he asked, concern

clouding his features.

"Y-Yeah. I-I'll be right back," Shade said.

She whirled around and rushed from her den. Once outside, she started to run. She sprinted through the forest, the rain stinging her eyes and branches whipping in her face. Her fur was soaked, but she kept going. She weaved through trees and leapt over logs, not caring where she was going. Finally, she slowed to a stop. She looked around her, panting. She'd run all the way to the stream. As her breathing slowed, she closed her eyes. The rain was soothing on her back, and she sat down. She closed her eyes. The run had done her good. But she had to get back. Oak might go looking for her. She sighed and got up.

Nothing was easy.

As Shade wandered back to her den, she couldn't help but wonder. *If I… like him… then does he like me?* She shook the thought off. *He'd better not. The sooner I can stop feeling like this, the better. He'd just make things more complicated.* Once more, frustration at Oak crept through her. She wished he would just leave her alone. She picked up the pace, hurrying through the wet underbrush. When she came to the tunnel of her den, she took a deep breath. She couldn't lose her temper with him again.

She slunk inside, shaking the water out of her fur. Oak looked up. She could tell that he was about to question her.

"Where were you? I was worried." He certainly sounded like it. Shade tried not to get annoyed. He was being too protective.

"I… went on a walk." She didn't want him to think that she had run away.

"Are you okay?" he inquired.

I am not *okay*, she thought. But if she said that, he'd just ask more questions.

"Yeah. I'm fine," she lied. He seemed relieved, but she wasn't sure if she was glad or not. She pawed awkwardly at the ground. Was he going to stay?

"It's a little cold," he pointed out needlessly. "Could I… maybe… stay for the night?"

Shade stared. Had he just read her mind?

"Uh-Umm…Sure," she stuttered. What was

she supposed to say? She glanced over at Oak. He seemed serious. She just hoped that he stayed on the other side of her den.

"Thank you," he said.

"You're welcome," she murmured. As she curled up against one wall of her small shelter, she heard Oak settle down beside her. Close, but not touching.

Shade slowly blinked open her eyes. Warmth pressed up against her back, and she shifted to see Oak lying beside her. He was still asleep, and his chest rose and fell in time to his breathing. She sighed inwardly. He seemed so helpless.

Since she had first set eyes on him, she'd never realized just how thin he was. *He must*

not be able to hunt very well. She'd never
smelled the scent of prey on him before, and,
other than the ones she had given him, he had
no scars. She already had many scars, and she
had guessed that he was around the same age
as her. She began to wonder if he was even a
wildcat. Had he simply escaped, just like her?
Maybe, but probably more recently. She
suddenly dreaded the time when she would
send him away. He could die. But if he had
survived this long…

"I just don't know anymore," she whispered
under her breath. It was hopeless. She had to
make a decision. Just then, Oak stirred. Shade
turned her attention back to him. He sat up and
turned to face her.

"Good morning, Shade," he greeted her. She tried not to smile. There was no way she would turn him away.

Chapter Eleven

Stars

"You did it! Good catch." Shade ran to Oak's side.

He struggled to speak through a mouthful of fur.

"Fanksh," he mumbled. His eyes shone with pride at his first catch. Shade had spent almost the entire day teaching Oak how to hunt. She was glad that her effort had finally paid off.

"Well…Now what do I do?" Oak asked.

"Eat it, of course!" she said.

He dropped the mouse on the ground and took a bite. He seemed to light up, and he immediately took another. Oak devoured the mouse in seconds before he straightened up, a delighted expression on his face.

"That was *delicious*!" he exclaimed. A tuft of fur was stuck to his lip. Shade tried not to laugh. That was exactly how Thunder had looked when he'd had his first mouse.

"I'm glad you like it," she told him.

"Now I have something to show you," Oak said. He began to lead Shade towards the cliff. She hesitated for a moment.

"Come on!" he called over his shoulder.

Shade dashed up to him, stopping beside

him. He continued to walk up the mountain, completely silent as they made their way through the trees. Shade began to grow curious. She'd already been on the cliff before. How could he know more about the cliff than her? The only other time he'd been there was when she found him in her territory, and he hadn't mentioned anything about that night.

Just as the sun slipped out of sight, they reached the top. Shade looked around. The view from the cliff was even more amazing with the sun's dying rays illuminating the forest. The sky was a stunning rainbow of orange, pink, purple, and blue, with wispy clouds floating dreamily overhead. Oak moved beside her, startling her out of her trance.

"Is this what you wanted to show me?" Shade asked. He shook his head.

"No. Just a few more minutes, and you'll see," he said.

Shade sat down. Until it was time, she was content to simply watch the sky as it turned to even more beautiful hues. She sat in total silence, not doing, not thinking, just being. The cold seemed to disappear as Shade slipped more and more into her mind. Her thoughts drifted by like the clouds in the sky. They never lingered, merely floating around for a few seconds before being wisped away by the breeze of emptiness. Shade stayed in her reverie for what could have been hours, or minutes, until Oak nudged her gently on the shoulder. She turned to face him, blinking the faraway look out of her eyes. Oak smiled softly at her. She couldn't help but smile back.

"Lay down, and close your eyes," he whispered to her. She obeyed, but kept her eyes open a slit to watch him settle beside her. "Then turn on your back and tilt your head up."

Cautiously, she rolled onto her back. She knew how dangerous it was for a cat to expose their stomach. She waited a few moments before she tilted her head to the sky.

"You can open your eyes now," he said. She slowly blinked them open.

A thrill ran through her. Stars covered the sky, spots of light shining forth through the velvety darkness. A thick band of the dazzling lights wound its way across the sky, a shimmering wave of light and color. Bright orbs of brilliance stood out among the glow of the smaller stars. Shade gasped.

"Oh…" she breathed. She couldn't take her eyes off of the heavenly spectacle. In the corner of her eye, she could see Oak turn his head to look at her.

"Do you like it?" he asked. She pried herself away from the magnificent sight to look at him directly.

"It's…amazing," she said. He glanced back up at the sky.

"It really is… isn't it," he sighed.

Shade was surprised at his broken-hearted tone. She wondered why the stars meant so much to him.

"Are you okay?" she asked. He sighed again and closed his eyes.

"When I was a very young kitten, my mother used to tell me stories about the stars. She told me that they were the spirits of every cat who passed. She said that they were our ancestors, and our past. She said that my three brothers were up there, waiting for us to join them. She always sounded so sad when she talked about my siblings. I was, too. When I was young, I wanted to go out on my own and find the place where the stars met the earth. She talked about that, too. She said it was a magical place where you could be with anyone, in this world or not. But it disappears in the day. The stars melt away, and the spirits drift off to the sky." His voice tightened. "It was my goal, my sole purpose in life, to reach that place."

"But I couldn't leave my mother. She was getting old, and sickly. The day she died, I promised on her behalf that I would find where the stars touch the ground, and we would all be together. The day after our people took her body away, I escaped. Ever since, I've been trying to get there. To the magical place. Every night, I would lie on the ground and gaze at the stars until I fell asleep. But no matter how far I went, I never arrived.

"I began to starve. I survived on carrion and roadkill, and I sheltered on the side of the road, hoping an understanding person would take me in. I went on like that until the day I saw you. I could tell from the start that you knew how to care for yourself. I just hoped you could care for me." He paused and opened his eyes.

"I could have left you alone after the first time we met, but I couldn't give up. I tracked you down. I crossed the stream in the night, when the ice had frozen over completely, and I found your den. As I was hanging over that cliff, I thought it was the end. But, no. You rescued me. In that moment, I knew that where the spirits walk wasn't a place. It was a feeling." He looked her in the eye.

"Shade, you are what I've been waiting for. You helped me learn that in order to connect with the spirits, you need to connect with yourself. You made me realize that. I'd been spending my days searching for something that was already there. You make me feel happy. You make me feel good." He gazed at her intensely. "Shade…I think it's time I told you…I…love you." The way he said it made Shade's heart leap. All the feelings she'd had about him came flooding forth in a whirlpool of compassion.

"I love you, too," she said.

The heavens above seemed to grow brighter with every second. Shade's heart pounded as she leaned forward. Oak copied her movement. Shade made the first stroke of love with her tongue, right on his heart.

Epilogue

Shade stood at the edge of the cliff. Oak lay, still asleep, in her den. The sun rose in front of her, casting its light over the mountains. The wind blew, ruffling her fur, and the forest below her swayed with it. The land was a patchwork of dark and light green trees, with the stream burbling peacefully in the center of it all. Shade closed her eyes in pure happiness, letting the wind whistle blissfully around her. She tilted her face to the sky and let the warmth of the sun soak into her. She opened her eyes, and felt a ripple of power spread through her. Confidence, bravery, kindness, and love. That was what she felt. As she gazed around the magnificent woods, she knew. This was Shade's Forest.

Acknowledgements

A very loving thanks to my mom, Lauren, and my dad, Thomas. Without you, this book would not have been possible. Thank you for supporting me and encouraging me to pursue my dreams of writing and for being there every step of the way. You are the best parents anyone could ask for.

Thanks to my cousin, Julia, for always giving me a good laugh, and my grandma, Nenna, for giving great advice. Thank you both for caring so much.

I especially appreciate my amazing fifth grade teacher, Mrs. Budman, for being so kind and understanding. You helped me a lot.

To my close friends, Luca, Marjie, and Tracy, thank you so much for reading and re-reading my book. Thank you to Jack, May, Luca, Daniel, Catherine, Bhakti, and Kennedy for being good friends and supporting me through this process.

I'm grateful to the Hockley family for celebrating this success with me and supporting me with words of encouragement.

I'm so glad that I had this wonderful opportunity of being a published author, so thank you to the publishing company, ReadyAimWrite Kids, and to Stephen Kozan, for seeing the potential in my Flash Fiction writing. Thanks to the illustrator for creating the beautiful cover.

Lastly, much love and thanks to Hamilton, my cat, for inspiring me and comforting me when things were tough. I miss you, and I hope that you are happy.

This book is my dream come true, and I couldn't have done it without the help and effort of all of you. Thank you.